HOME REPAIR AND IMPROVEMENT

CLOSETS, SPACE, AND STORAGE

9/98

TIME® LIFE BOOKS

OTHER PUBLICATIONS:

DO IT YOURSELF
Total Golf
How to Fix It
The Time-Life Complete Gardener
The Art of Woodworking

COOKING
Weight Watchers® Smart Choice Recipe Collection
Great Taste/Low Fat
Williams-Sonoma Kitchen Library

HISTORY
Our American Century
What Life was Like
The American Story
Voices of the Civil War
The American Indians
Lost Civilizations
Mysteries of the Unknown
Time Frame
The Civil War
Cultural Atlas

TIME-LIFE KIDS
Student Library
Library of First Questions and Answers
A Child's First Library of Learning
I Love Math
Nature Company Discoveries
Understanding Science & Nature

SCIENCE/NATURE
Voyage Through the Universe

For information on and a full description
of any of the Time-Life Books series listed above,
please call 1-800-621-7026 or write:

Reader Information
Time-Life Customer Service
P.O. Box C-32068
Richmond Virginia 23261-2068

HOME REPAIR AND IMPROVEMENT

CLOSETS, SPACE, AND STORAGE

BY THE EDITORS OF TIME-LIFE BOOKS, ALEXANDRIA, VIRGINIA

The Consultants

Jon Arno, a wood technologist residing in Michigan, where he works for a family lumber business, is known for his skills in furniture design and cabinetmaking. Mr. Arno has written extensively on the properties and uses of wood and is the author of *The Woodworkers Visual Handbook* and a frequent contributor to *Fine Woodworking* magazine. He also conducts seminars on wood identification and early American furniture design.

Stewart McLaughlin has been working in the design and renovation field for 17 years. Trained as a graphic artist, Mr. McLaughlin specializes in the design and layout of cabinets and built-ins.

CONTENTS

Creative Closets

1

Storage problems in a home can often be solved by taking advantage of previously overlooked space. Existing closets can be arranged more efficiently with custom-built organizing systems, or converted into hobby centers or moth-proof vaults. And with a minimum of expense, you can add a closet to a room or transform unused areas under staircases or behind attic kneewalls into capacious cabinets.

Framing a kneewall closet →

Custom-building a closet-organizing system like the one on these pages allows you to size and arrange components to suit your needs. The boxes, shelves, and racks can be positioned in a variety of ways to accommodate men's, women's, or children's clothing.

Sizing Components: The systems shown here are sized to fit a typical bedroom closet, which is generally 5 to 6 feet long, 2 feet deep, and 8 feet high, but you can adapt the measurements to work in almost any space. In all cases, however, hang clothes rods 9 inches away from the wall and allow about 66 inches of room below them for women's dresses; give men's shirts, folded pants, and jackets at least 36 inches.

In these closets, shelf boxes are 12- by 12- by 9 inches; the stacking units have rabbets cut around the top edges *(page 12, Step 6)* so they will interlock. Footwear racks with hinged lids are 12 inches wide, 24 inches long, 3 inches high in front, and 6 inches high at the back. The two accessory racks are 12 inches wide, 2 inches deep, and $81\frac{1}{2}$ inches tall.

 TOOLS

Table saw
C-clamps
Bar clamps
Router
Rabbeting bit
Wood chisel
Mallet
Electric drill
Countersink bit
Screwdriver bit
Hammer
Nail set
Hand roller
Utility knife
Electronic stud finder
Carpenter's level
Hacksaw
Carpenter's square
Plumb bob

 **MATERIALS**

1 x 1s, 1 x 2s, 2 x 4
Furniture-grade
  plywood ($\frac{3}{4}$")
Hardboard ($\frac{1}{4}$")
Wood dowels ($\frac{1}{2}$")
Wood trim ($\frac{1}{4}$" x 1")
Quarter-round molding
Picture-frame molding
Edge banding
Wood screws ($\frac{1}{2}$" No. 5,
  $1\frac{1}{4}$", $1\frac{1}{2}$", 2" No. 8)

Finishing nails ($\frac{3}{4}$")
Brass "S" hooks
Drawer pulls
Catch ($\frac{3}{4}$" x $\frac{3}{4}$")
Piano hinge
Sliding-door hardware
Clothes rod and shelf
  brackets
Adjustable clothes rod
Sandpaper (medium
  grade)
Wood glue

 SAFETY TIPS

Wear goggles to protect your eyes when operating a power tool or driving nails.

A closet-organizing system.

In this sample arrangement, the shelf boxes at the right take up a small portion of the space for the hanging clothes. Drawers inserted into every second box store articles such as socks and undergarments. Boxes are also mounted at the top of the closet to house less frequently used items. A pair of footwear racks are situated to leave the left-hand corner of the floor empty for other uses. Accessory racks fitted with dowels and brass hooks for ties, belts, and other items hang from sliding-door hardware and travel along runners on the floor. When not in use, they are stored in the left-hand corner, close to the front wall. A combination clothes-rod-and-shelf spans the length of the closet.

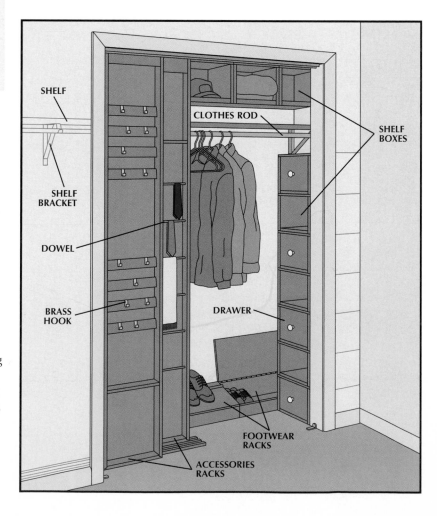

SHELF
SHELF BRACKET
DOWEL
BRASS HOOK
CLOTHES ROD
SHELF BOXES
DRAWER
FOOTWEAR RACKS
ACCESSORIES RACKS

A shelf-and-drawer system.

The closet at left contains the same components as the one opposite, but they are arranged to provide more room for items hanging from the clothes rod. This layout can also be used to divide the closet for two users. The floor boxes are arranged in two short stacks placed at the back of the closet, and the footwear racks flank the boxes. The sliding accessories racks are shown in their hidden position behind the closet framing.

A centered organizing system.

In the closet at right, two clothes rods and two pairs of wall-mounted shelf boxes at each side of the closet span its width, rather than its length. Footwear racks are positioned against the closet's side walls, leaving the middle of the space free for a tall stack of boxes and for the accessories racks, which slide outward instead of side-to-side.

BUILDING SHELF BOXES

ROUTING DADOES AND RABBETS

Wooden furniture derives much of its structural stability from its joints. To lock the components of a piece together, two special router cuts are often used. A rabbet *(below, Step 1)*—a stepped cut along the edge or end of a piece—fortifies corner joints. A dado *(opposite, Step 2)*—a rectangular channel cut across a panel—sometimes holds the back or bottom of a box or drawer to the sides, and secures fixed shelves in the sides of a piece.

The best tool to make these cuts is a router. Rab-

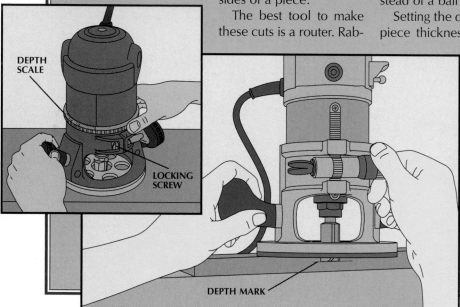

DEPTH SCALE

LOCKING SCREW

DEPTH MARK

bets can be cut with two types of bits. Piloted rabbeting bits come with a set of ball-bearing guides in varying diameters; the guide you install on the bit determines the width of the cut. As you move the router to make the rabbet, the guide rolls along the adjoining surface, keeping the bit from wandering off-line. An alternative is a straight bit, which can also cut dadoes; with this bit, the router is guided by a straight edge instead of a ball bearing.

Setting the depth of cut—usually one half the workpiece thickness—varies with different routers. For a tool with a depth scale, place the router on the piece, loosen the locking screw, and turn the motor unit clockwise until the tip of the bit contacts the wood *(inset)*. Set the depth scale to zero, then move the router so the bit overhangs the edge of the wood. Lower the bit until the depth scale registers the desired depth, then tighten the locking screw. If the router has no depth scale, mark the depth of cut on the edge of the piece, then turn the adjustment screw to lower the bit until it aligns with the depth mark *(left)*.

1. Plowing rabbets.

◆ For each shelf box, cut two 9- by 12-inch sides, one $11\frac{1}{8}$- by 12-inch top, one $8\frac{5}{8}$- by $11\frac{1}{8}$-inch back, and an $11\frac{1}{8}$- by $11\frac{1}{8}$-inch bottom from $\frac{3}{4}$-inch furniture-grade plywood.

◆ Mark lines for rabbets $\frac{3}{4}$ inch from the top and back edges of each side piece, and $\frac{3}{4}$ inch from the back edge of the top piece.

◆ Clamp one piece securely to a worktable, protecting the surface with wood pads.

◆ In a router, install a piloted rabbeting bit fitted with a bearing for a $\frac{3}{4}$-inch rabbet.

◆ Hold the router so the bit overhangs the edge of the board at one end. Turn on the motor and move the bit into the wood until the pilot bearing contacts the wood.

◆ Guide the router from left to right, pressing the bearing against the edge *(right)* until you reach the end of the piece.

◆ Rout the remaining rabbets in the same way.

RABBET

PILOTED RABBETING BIT

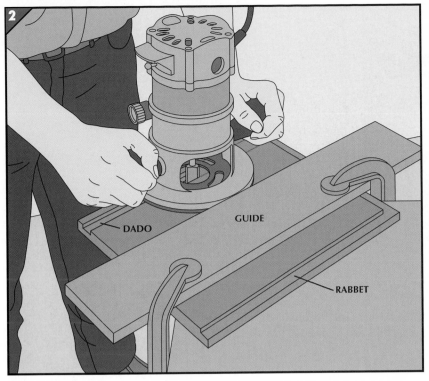

2. Cutting dadoes.

◆ Outline $\frac{3}{4}$-inch dadoes $\frac{1}{4}$ inch from the bottom edges of the sides and back pieces, then set one of the pieces on the worktable.

◆ Install a $\frac{3}{4}$-inch straight bit in the router, then set the tool down so the bit is aligned with the outline.

◆ Butt a straight board as a guide against the router's base. Ensure that the guide is parallel to the outline, then clamp it to the workpiece.

◆ Set the depth of cut—$\frac{3}{8}$ inch in $\frac{3}{4}$-inch plywood—then, starting at one end of the piece, rout the dado with the tool riding along the guide (above).

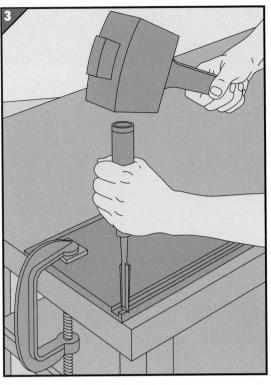

3. Notching for trim pieces.

On each side piece, make a $\frac{1}{4}$-inch notch to hold the trim piece (page 12, Step 5): At the bottom front corner, cut the outer wall of the dado to the same depth as the channel with a wood chisel and a mallet (above).

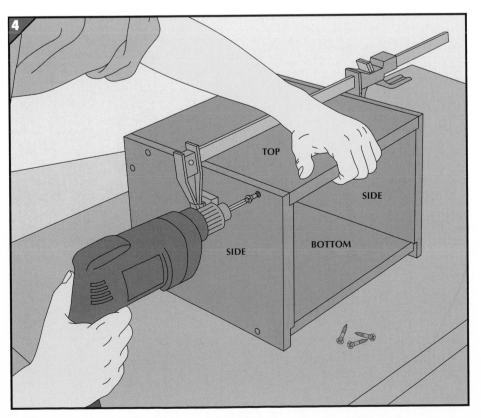

4. Assembling the boxes.

◆ Fit the top piece in its rabbets in the sides, secure the assembly with a bar clamp across the top, then slide the bottom into its dadoes in the sides and back piece.

◆ Drill five countersunk holes for $1\frac{1}{4}$-inch No. 8 wood screws through each side piece—two into the top and back pieces and one into the bottom—then drive the screws (left).

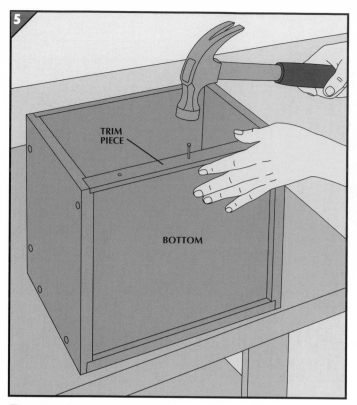

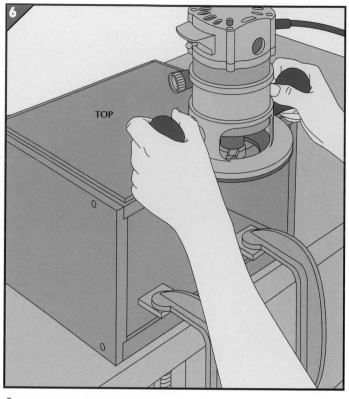

5. Adding bottom trim.

◆ Cut a length of $\frac{1}{4}$- by 1-inch wood trim to fit at the bottom front of each box.

◆ Set the box on its back and tack the trim to the edge of the bottom with three $\frac{3}{4}$-inch finishing nails—one near each end and one in between *(above)*.

◆ Sink the nailheads below the surface with a nail set.

6. Routing the box tops.

For each box to be stacked, rout rabbets at the perimeter of the top so it will interlock with the unit placed on top of it.

◆ Clamp the box to the worktable, then fit a router with a piloted rabbeting bit for a $\frac{3}{8}$-inch-wide cut. Rout the rabbet along the sides and back.

◆ Switch to a bearing for a $\frac{1}{4}$-inch rabbet and cut a narrower recess along the front *(above)*.

7. Applying edge banding.

◆ Place the box on its back and set a household iron to HIGH (without steam).

◆ Cut a strip of edge banding slightly longer than the area to be covered and position the strip with the adhesive side down so any excess hangs over the outside of the box.

◆ Spread a rag on the banding to prevent burn marks, then run the hot iron slowly along it *(right),* moving from the middle toward the ends to keep the banding from slipping and leaving gaps at joints.

◆ Applying even pressure, run a hand roller or a wood block back and forth along the edge.

◆ After the glue has set, trim off excess banding with a utility knife.

◆ Smooth the edges with medium-grade sandpaper.

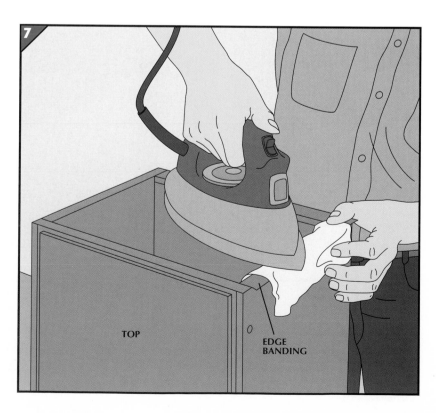

MAKING DRAWERS

Anatomy of a shelf-box drawer.
A shelf-box drawer is sized to fit inside a shelf box with $\frac{1}{8}$ inch of clearance at the sides and top. As with the boxes, the drawer back and front fit into rabbets cut in the side pieces. The bottom sits in dadoes $\frac{1}{4}$ inch from the bottoms of the side and back pieces. A false front, cut 1 inch taller than the drawer, is fastened to the front piece, and a drawer pull is anchored to both pieces.

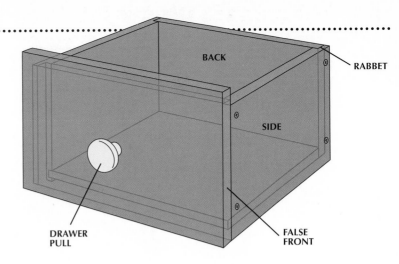

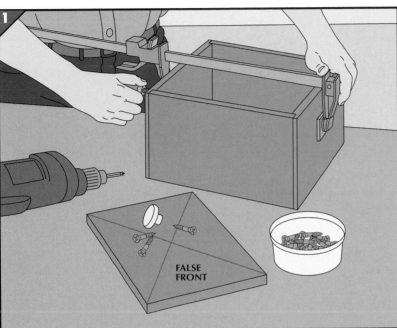

1. Assembling the drawers.
◆ Cut the drawer parts to size, then rabbet *(page 10)* the front and back edges of the sides and rout dadoes *(page 11)* along the back and sides to accommodate the bottom.
◆ Locate the center of the false front by marking intersecting diagonal lines on its front between opposite corners.
◆ Fit the sides, front, back, and bottom together and secure the assembly with a bar clamp *(left)*.
◆ Drill a countersunk hole for a $1\frac{1}{4}$-inch No. 8 wood screw at each corner of the sides into the front and back, but drive in only the screws at the back.

2. Attaching the drawer front.
◆ Lay the false front face-down on the worktable and set the drawer assembly on top, aligning the bottoms of the drawer front and false front with a straight board.
◆ Draw a line along the top of the drawer on the back of the false front *(right)*.
◆ Remove the bar clamp and detach the drawer front from the sides. Realign the drawer front and false front, clamp the pieces to the table face-down, and fasten them together with four $1\frac{1}{4}$-inch No. 8 wood screws, driving the fasteners through the drawer front into the false front at each corner.
◆ Reassemble the pieces and drive screws through the sides into the front.
◆ To attach the drawer pull, drill a hole for the screw through the false front and drawer front at the center mark, then line up the handle with the hole and tighten the screw.

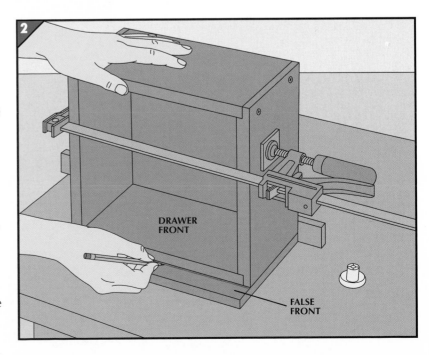

MOUNTING BOXES ON A WALL

1. Positioning the boxes.

◆ With a stud finder, locate and mark the stud locations on the closet's back wall.

◆ Mark a level line along the back wall 66 inches from the floor to position the shelf above the clothes rod.

◆ Draw a second level line 9 inches higher for the bottoms of the shelf boxes *(right)*.

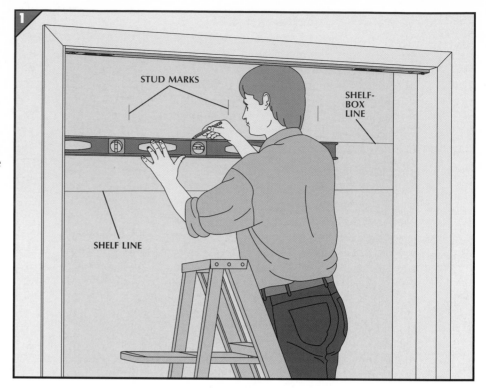

2. Hanging the boxes.

◆ Build shelf boxes *(pages 10-12)* in pairs, omitting the stacking rabbets around the top.

◆ Mark and drill two countersunk pilot holes for $1\frac{1}{4}$-inch No. 8 wood screws through the side of one box. Clamp the units together and bore corresponding holes into the side of another box, then drive the screws *(above, left)*.

◆ Nail a board to the wall studs as a support cleat so its top edge aligns with the shelf-box line; then, propping the first pair of boxes on the cleat, fasten them to the wall, driving two 2-inch screws through the back of each box at the stud marks.

◆ Mount the remaining pairs of boxes the same way *(above, right)*, installing each set flush against the previous one. Remove the cleat.

FASHIONING FOOTWEAR RACKS

Anatomy of a footwear rack.

The footwear rack at right consists of two tapered side pieces—$11\frac{1}{4}$ inches long, 6 inches high at the back and 3 inches high in the front—joined to a 6- by 24-inch back and a 3- by 24-inch front. The sides fit in $\frac{3}{4}$-inch rabbets cut at each end of the front and back pieces. The top of the rack consists of a $10\frac{3}{4}$- by 24-inch lid joined by a piano hinge to a $1\frac{3}{4}$- by 24-inch hinge strap. The lid overhangs the front by $\frac{5}{8}$ inch, creating a lip for easy lifting. A piece of quarter-round molding serves as a heel catch.

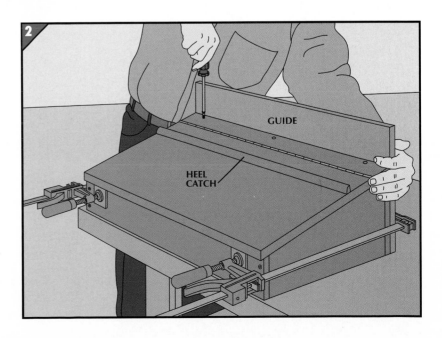

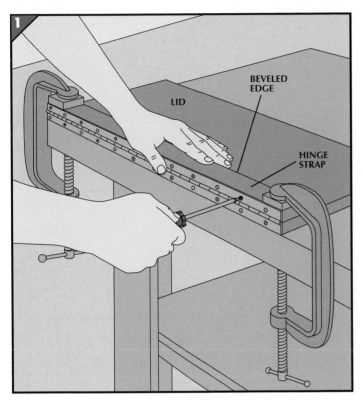

1. Hinging the lid.

◆ Cut the pieces to size, then rout rabbets *(page 10)* in each end of the front and back pieces to accommodate the sides.
◆ Cut 15-degree bevels *(page 61, Step 1)* along the top edges of the front and back pieces, and bevel the back edge of the hinge strap.
◆ Fasten the front and back pieces to the sides with $1\frac{1}{4}$-inch No. 8 wood screws, driving two into each joint.
◆ With a hacksaw, cut a length of piano hinge slightly shorter than the width of the lid.
◆ Place the lid on a work surface and lay the hinge strap on top of it, then attach the bottom leaf of the hinge to the lid with a $\frac{1}{2}$-inch No. 5 screw at each end. Drive a screw through every second hole, then fasten the top hinge leaf to the strap in the same way *(left)*.

2. Attaching the top.

◆ Cut a piece of quarter-round molding to the length of the rack, and position it as a heel catch on the top piece about 2 inches from the hinge so the round side is facing the front. Making sure the catch is parallel to the front and back, fasten it to the top with three 1-inch finishing nails.
◆ Secure a piece of scrap plywood as a guide to the back of the rack with bar clamps.
◆ Set the lid on the rack flush against the guide, then drill three countersunk holes for $1\frac{1}{4}$-inch No. 8 wood screws, one 2 inches from each end and one in between, through the hinge strap and into the back piece.
◆ Drive a screw into each hole *(right)*.

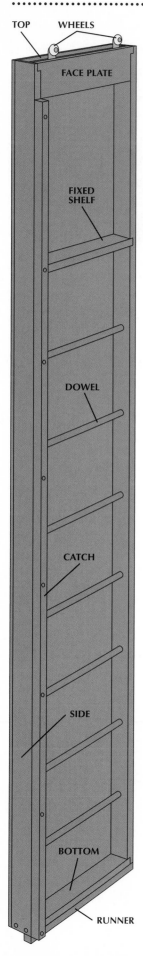

TOP WHEELS

FACE PLATE

FIXED SHELF

DOWEL

CATCH

SIDE

BOTTOM

RUNNER

Accessory racks.

Two sliding racks provide storage for ties, belts, scarves, and other small accessories. The dowel rack at left fits behind the one that has slats and brass hooks *(opposite)*. Its side pieces are 2 inches wide and $81\frac{1}{2}$ inches tall. The top and bottom, which fit in $\frac{3}{4}$-inch rabbets cut in the side pieces, are $11\frac{1}{8}$ inches long; the bottom is the same width as the sides, but the top is $\frac{3}{4}$ inch wide to allow for a notched face plate to which the wheels are attached. A $\frac{1}{4}$-inch hardboard back is fastened to the sides, top, and bottom, and a fixed shelf sits in dadoes in the sides at a convenient height. Wood dowels $\frac{1}{2}$ inch in diameter and $11\frac{1}{8}$ inches long fit in holes drilled in the sides at 8-inch intervals. The wheels roll in door-track hardware mounted on a hanging rail, and a foot-long 1-by-1 runner fastened to the bottom of the rack slides between guides on the floor of the closet. A $\frac{3}{4}$-by-$\frac{3}{4}$-inch catch fastened along the front left edge of the rack contacts a matching catch on the back of the slat rack, pulling the dowel rack into view as the slat rack is pulled out. Nearly identical to the dowel rack, the slat rack has brass hooks and slats instead of dowels, and its top is 2 inches wide since the wheels are mounted on the back rather than on the face plate.

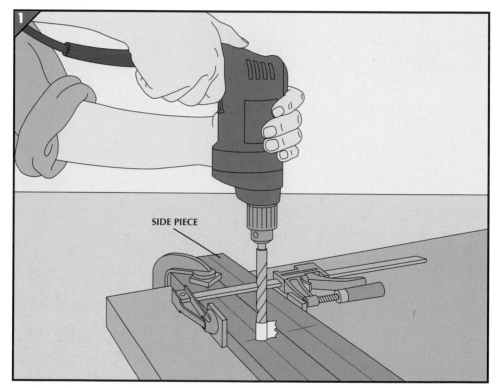

SIDE PIECE

1. Assembling the dowel rack.

◆ Cut all the parts of the rack, then mark a line down the middle of each side piece.

◆ Clamp the sides edge-to-edge with their ends aligned and, with a carpenter's square, mark lines across them for the shelf dado. Then, starting from the bottom end, make a mark every 8 inches for the dowels.

◆ Fit an electric drill with a $\frac{1}{2}$-inch bit and wrap a strip of masking tape around it $\frac{3}{8}$ inch from the tip to mark the depth.

◆ Drill a hole into the side pieces at each point where a dowel line intersects a center line, stopping when the tape contacts the wood *(above)*.

◆ Rout rabbets *(page 10)* along the top and bottom of the sides and $\frac{3}{4}$-inch dadoes *(page 11)* at the shelf lines, then fasten the top, bottom, and shelf to one side with $1\frac{1}{4}$-inch No. 8 wood screws. Fit the dowels into their holes, then add the opposite side.

2. Building the slat version.

◆ Cut all the parts of the rack—excepting the slats—then assemble it as you did the dowel version, omitting the dowels.

◆ For each rack, cut a back panel of $\frac{1}{4}$-inch hardboard to the outside dimensions of the unit.

◆ Center the slat rack over its back on a worktable, then outline the inner edges of the rack on the back. Mark a level line across the back at each desired slat location, leaving the width of two slats between lines.

◆ For each slat, cut a length of picture-frame molding to fit within the outline, apply wood glue to the back of the slat, then clamp it to the back along one of the lines *(right)*. Turn the panel onto one side and drive two $\frac{1}{2}$-inch No. 5 screws through the panel into the slat.

◆ Fasten the remaining slats this way.

◆ Attach back panels to both racks by laying the unit face-down, applying wood glue to its edges, and setting the panel in place. Drive 1-inch No. 8 wood screws every 16 inches through the back panel into the rack.

◆ Hang flat brass "S" hooks *(photograph)* from the slats as shown on page 8.

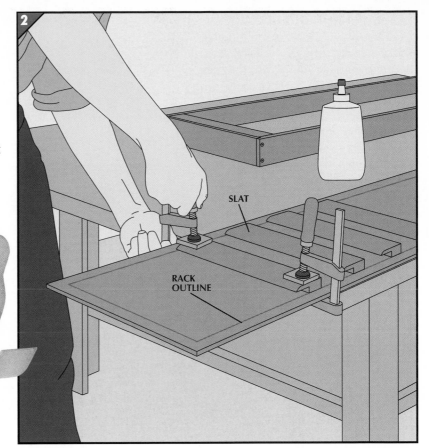

3. Adding the wheels and face plates.

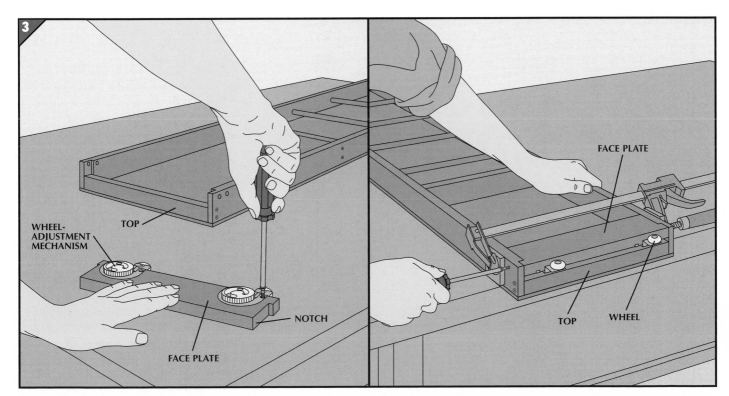

◆ Cut $\frac{3}{8}$- by $1\frac{5}{8}$-inch notches at the ends of each face plate.

◆ For the dowel rack, attach a door-track wheel to the face plate, with the screws supplied, along the unnotched edge $\frac{1}{2}$ inch from each end *(above, left)*. For the slat rack, attach the wheels to the back of the rack so the top of the wheel-adjustment mechanism is flush with the top of the unit.

◆ For each rack, clamp the face plate across the front of the unit flush with the top, then fasten the plate to the sides with countersunk $1\frac{1}{4}$-inch screws *(above, right)*.

4. Adding catches and runners.

◆ On the back rack—here, the dowel version—clamp one of the catches to the front left edge, flush with the bottom of the unit.

◆ Drill countersunk holes for $1\frac{1}{4}$-inch screws through the catch and into the rack at 6-inch intervals, then fasten the catch in place *(right)*.

◆ Screw the second catch to the front rack on the back right edge.

◆ On the dowel rack, fasten the runner with a pair of screws to the bottom, flush with the front edge *(inset)*. Attach the runner along the back edge of the slat rack.

◆ Trim both of the racks with edge banding *(page 12)*.

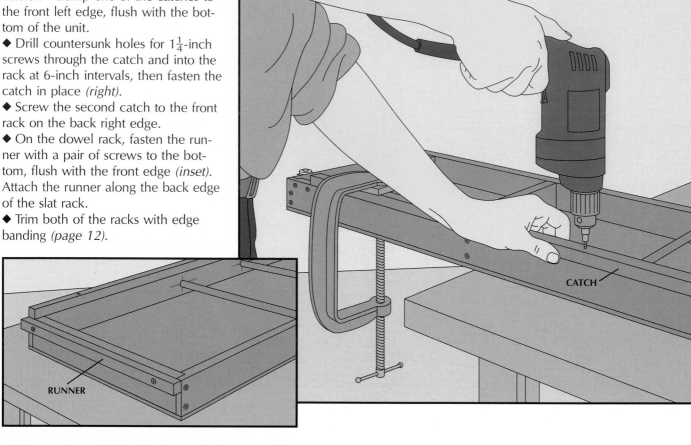

CATCH

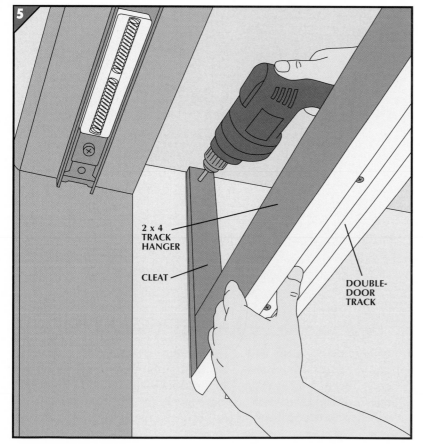

RUNNER

5. Mounting the door-track hardware.

◆ Cut a 2-by-4 hanger for the hardware $1\frac{1}{2}$ inch shorter than the length of the closet. Attach a 4-foot length of double-door track to one edge of the hanger, flush with one end, using the screws supplied.

◆ Measure from the bottom of the runner on one of the racks to the top of the wheels, add 1 inch to the distance, and transfer the result to the closet side walls, 3 inches in from the front wall, measuring from the floor. With a plumb bob and a carpenter's square, extend the marks to the ceiling.

◆ Cut two 1-by-2 cleats to fit between the ceiling and the marks on the wall, then screw one to each end of the track hanger with a pair of $1\frac{1}{2}$-inch screws so the bottom end of the cleat is flush with the bottom edge of the hanger.

◆ Working with a helper, hold up the hanger assembly so the tops of the cleats sit against the ceiling and the outer edges align with the lines on the side walls. If the hanger aligns with a stud behind the wall, fasten each cleat just below the ceiling with a $1\frac{1}{2}$-inch screw *(left)*, and add a second screw 1 inch above the 2-by-4. If there are no studs behind the cleats, use hollow-wall anchors instead of screws.

2 x 4 TRACK HANGER

CLEAT

DOUBLE-DOOR TRACK

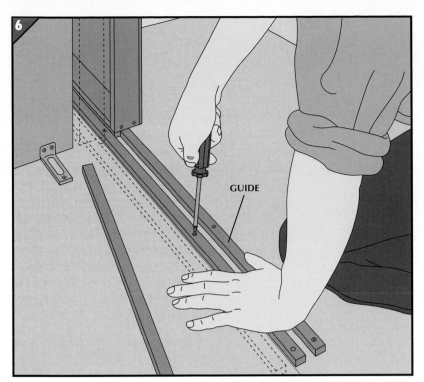

6. Installing the guides.

◆ From 1-by-1 lumber, cut three 4-foot-long guides.
◆ Hang the back rack from the door track. Then, with a helper holding the rack plumb against the side wall, position a guide against the inner edge of the runner at the bottom of the rack.
◆ Checking that the guide is square, mark its outline on the floor.
◆ Counterbore holes for $1\frac{1}{4}$-inch screws through the guide at 10-inch intervals, reposition it on the floor, butting the end against the side wall, and fasten it down, sliding the rack out the way as necessary.
◆ Install the second guide this way, positioning it along the outer edge of the runner *(left)*.
◆ For the third guide, hang the front rack—represented by dashed lines in the illustration—and fasten the guide between the front-rack runner and the second guide.

TWO TYPES OF CLOTHES RODS

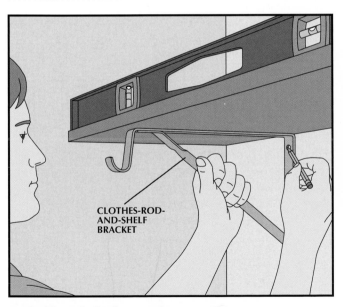

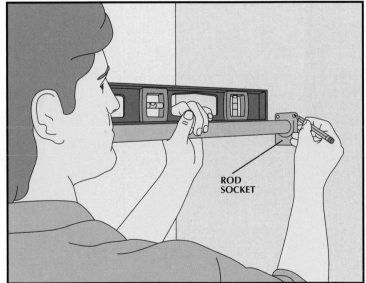

A shelf and clothes rod.

◆ Locate and mark the wall studs nearest the corners of the closet. Position a bracket plumb and level on one stud at an appropriate height for the clothing that will hang from the rod, then drive in the screws.
◆ Set one end of the shelf on the bracket, level the other end on the second bracket, and mark the screw holes over the the stud *(above)*.
◆ Remove the shelf and fasten the second bracket to the wall. To prevent a long shelf from sagging, add a third bracket at a stud between the first two.
◆ Hang an adjustable clothes rod from the brackets.

Installing a clothes rod.

◆ Screw a clothes-rod socket with the screws supplied to one side wall 9 inches from the back wall at a height suitable for the clothing that will hang on the rod. If there is no stud at the socket location, nail a cleat across the width of the closet to the studs, then attach the socket to the cleat.
◆ Insert one end of an adjustable clothes rod into the socket and slip the other socket on the other end of the pole.
◆ Holding a carpenter's level on the rod, extend the rod to the opposite side wall and adjust its height until it is level, then mark the screw holes *(above)*.
◆ Set the rod aside, fasten the second socket to the wall, and hang the rod.

An All-Purpose Hobby Cupboard

Hobbies such as sewing or model-making require a large, flat work surface and a place to store supplies. If your house has a limited amount of free space, you can replace an ordinary closet door with a hobby cupboard that tucks neatly away when not in use *(below)*. Choose a closet with ample space in front—one in a narrow hallway would lack sufficient area for the table. Finish the cabinet's back panel, which takes the place of the closet door, to match the other doors in the room.

Sizing the Cupboard: The cupboard on these pages fits a standard-size closet opening 32 inches wide and 80 inches tall. If the door you will be replacing has different dimensions, size the cabinet so the hardboard back is the same width as the opening but $1\frac{1}{4}$ inch narrower *(page 22, Step 3)* in order for the cupboard to close properly.

TOOLS

Table saw	Bar clamps	Mallet
Router	Hole-drilling jig	Hacksaw
Rabbeting bit	Electric drill	Utility knife
C-clamps	Screwdriver	Cold chisel
	Saber saw	Hammer
	Wood chisel	

MATERIALS

	Shelf pins	Hydraulic arm
1 x 2s, 2 x 2s	Wood glue	Hook-and-eye
Plywood ($\frac{3}{4}$")	Sandpaper	Door hinge
Hardboard ($\frac{1}{4}$")	(medium grade)	Glass-door hinges
Wood screws	Piano hinges	Door pull
($1\frac{1}{4}$" No. 8)	Furniture pins ($\frac{1}{2}$")	Ball-socket door
	Drop-leaf support	hardware

SAFETY TIPS

Protect your eyes with goggles when operating a power tool or chiseling a mortise.

Anatomy of a hobby cupboard.

This hobby cupboard has three sections—a door cabinet, a table, and a shelf unit—built of $\frac{3}{4}$-inch plywood and $\frac{1}{4}$-inch hardboard. In the door cabinet and shelf unit, the top and bottom pieces lock into rabbets *(page 10)* cut in the ends of the side pieces. The table—which includes a drop leaf—swings up against the front of the cabinet when not in use; it is attached with a piano hinge to a fixed double shelf set in dadoes *(page 11)* cut in the sides of the cabinet. A hydraulic arm facilitates the lifting of the table, and a hook-and-eye catch secures it in the closed position. Hinged to the underside of the table is a shelf unit; more storage is provided by cubbyholes in the upper section. Since the design precludes a regular door handle, a door pull and ball-socket hardware are used instead.

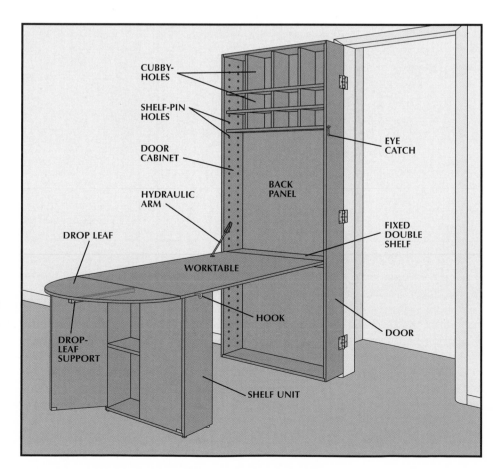

BUILDING THE DOOR CABINET

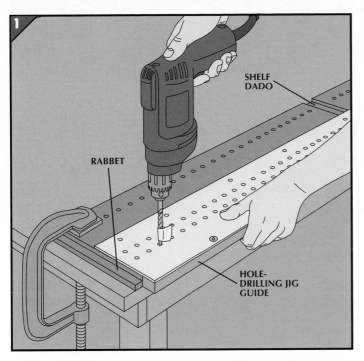

SHELF DADO

RABBET

HOLE-DRILLING JIG GUIDE

1. Preparing the door cabinet.

◆ Cut the plywood for the door cabinet: Make the side pieces 8 inches wide and 79 inches tall, and the top and bottom pieces $29\frac{3}{4}$ inches long.

◆ In the ends of the side pieces, rout $\frac{3}{4}$-inch-wide $\frac{3}{8}$-inch-deep rabbets (page 10). For the fixed double shelf, rout dadoes (page 11) $1\frac{1}{2}$ inches wide, with their top edges 29 inches from the bottom.

◆ Clamp one of the sides to a work surface inside-face up, protecting it with wood pads, and set a hole-drilling jig on it so one end aligns with the rabbet and the guide is against the edge.

◆ Fit a drill with a bit the size of the shelf pins you plan to use and mark the hole depth on the bit with masking tape—taking into account the thickness of the jig.

◆ Choosing one row of holes in the jig, drill the holes, stopping when the masking tape hits the jig. Reposition the jig as needed to finish the row of holes, then move it to the opposite side of the piece to bore the second row (left).

◆ Repeat the process to drill the shelf-pin holes in the other side piece.

TRICKS OF THE TRADE

A Simple Hole-Drilling Jig

In place of a commercial hole-drilling jig, you can use one made of a couple of 1-by-3s. Cut one piece 8 inches long to serve as a fence and the other as long as the cabinet side pieces to make an arm. Screw one face of the fence to one end of the arm, then draw a line down the center of the arm. Mark the center line at 1-inch intervals and drill a hole the same diameter as your shelf pins through the wood at each mark. To use the jig, hold the fence flush against the end of the workpiece at the appropriate distance from the edge and drill the holes.

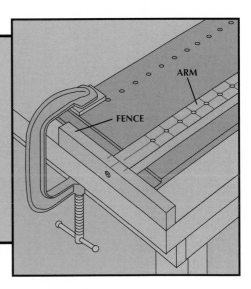

ARM

FENCE

MOUNTING CABINET SHELVES ON STANDARDS

CLIP

PILASTER

An alternative to drilling shelf-pin holes is to attach metal shelf standards. Horizontally-slotted standards, known as pilasters (left), are suitable for cabinets and bookcases. They can be nailed or screwed to the surface or recessed in dadoes. In either case, cut them to length with a hacksaw and smooth the edges with a file. Using a carpenter's level, mark the positions of all four standards on the side pieces. Attach one pair to one side and insert clips in the slots. Lay a shelf on the clips and level it, then have a helper fasten the other pair of standards to the opposite side of the cabinet.

2. Assembling the cabinet.

◆ Fit the bottom piece into the rabbets in the side pieces, drill pilot holes for three $1\frac{1}{4}$-inch No.8 wood screws through each side and into the bottom, and drive the screws.

◆ Fasten the top piece to the sides the same way.

◆ Make the fixed shelf by screwing two $29\frac{3}{4}$-inch-long pieces of $\frac{3}{4}$-inch plywood together face to face.

◆ Lay the cabinet on one side, then slide the shelf into its dadoes *(right)*.

◆ Attach the shelf to each side piece with three screws.

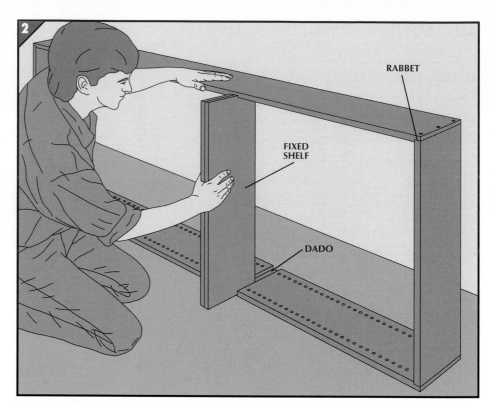

3. Attaching the back panel.

◆ Cut the back from $\frac{1}{4}$-inch hardboard as tall as the cabinet, but $1\frac{1}{4}$ inches wider. Also make "cauls" for clamping the panel: Cut two 2-by-2s about a foot longer than the panel, two more slightly shorter than its width, and four 1-by-2s about 3 feet long.

◆ Lay the cabinet face-down on two boards and apply wood glue along all the edges.

◆ Position the back on the cabinet so the $1\frac{1}{4}$ inches of extra width overhangs the side where the doorknob will be located, then secure the panel with bar clamps and the cauls, aligning the 2-by-2s with the edges of the unit and the 1-by-2s in a V pattern across the 2-by-2s *(above)*.

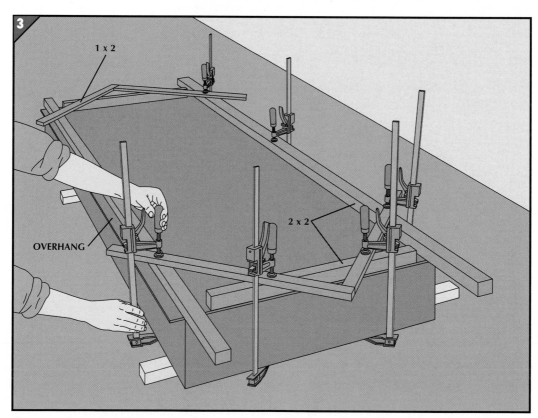

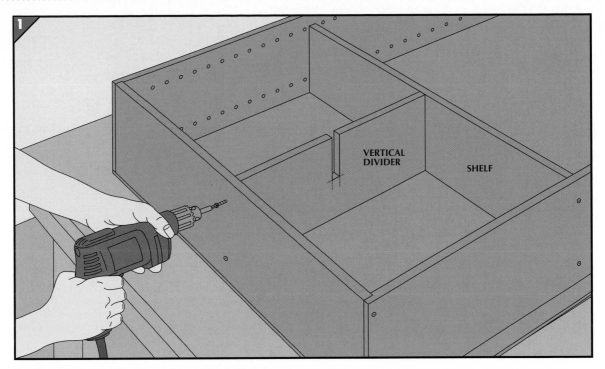

1. The bottom shelf and vertical divider.

◆ Cut the bottom cubbyhole shelf to fit snugly between the cabinet sides and the vertical divider to fit between the shelf and top; make both pieces 1 inch shallower than the depth of the cabinet.
◆ Mark a $\frac{3}{4}$-inch-wide slot across the middle of the divider from one edge halfway to the other edge. Cut the sides of the notch with a saber saw and remove the waste with a wood chisel.
◆ Screw the divider across the middle of the shelf at a 90-degree angle, forming a T.
◆ Lay the cabinet on its back and fit in the T. Screw the shelf to the sides, then screw the divider to the top *(above)*.

2. Adding the horizontal divider.

◆ Cut a second shelf as a horizontal divider and notch it as you did the vertical one.
◆ Fit the divider over the notch in the vertical divider *(right)*.
◆ Install as many cubbyholes as you wish by adding shelves and dividers, or install regular shelves later using shelf pins in the holes.

1. Cutting the tabletop.

◆ To make the large section of the table, cut a piece of plywood 48 inches long and $29\frac{3}{4}$ inches wide.

◆ For the drop leaf, trim a second piece $28\frac{3}{4}$ inches wide and at least 15 inches long *(right)*.

◆ Smooth the cut edges with medium-grade sandpaper.

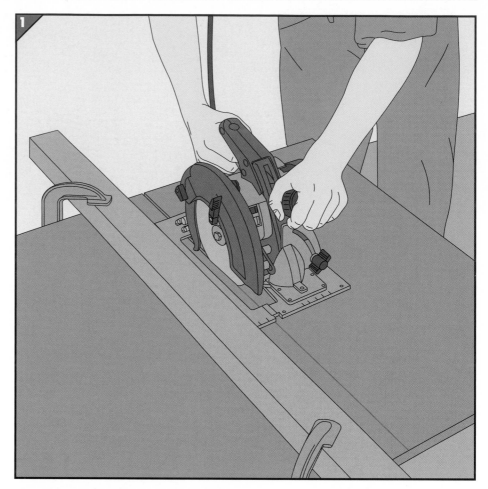

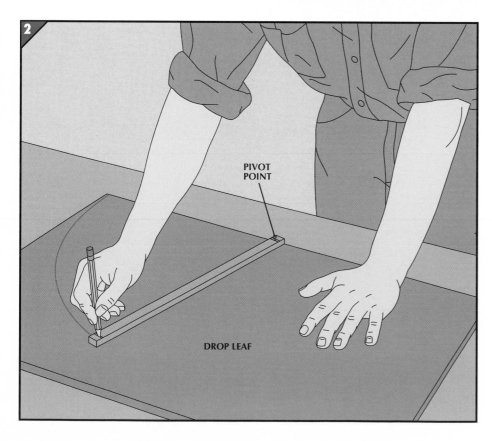

PIVOT POINT

DROP LEAF

2. Marking the drop leaf.

◆ On the drop-leaf section, mark the middle of one of the longer edges as a pivot point.

◆ Cut a scrap piece of wood $14\frac{3}{4}$ inches long and drill a counterbored hole through it $\frac{3}{8}$ inch from one end, large enough to fit the tip of a pencil. Tack the other end of the piece to the plywood at the pivot point so the end is flush with the edge.

◆ Fit a pencil in the hole in the wood strip and, starting at one corner, scribe an arc on the drop leaf *(left)*.

3. Cutting the arc.

◆ Clamp the drop leaf to a work surface so the arc overhangs the surface; protect the piece with wood pads.

◆ Starting at one corner, cut the arc with a saber saw. As you near the end of the cut, support the piece with your free hand (right) to avoid breaking the corner.

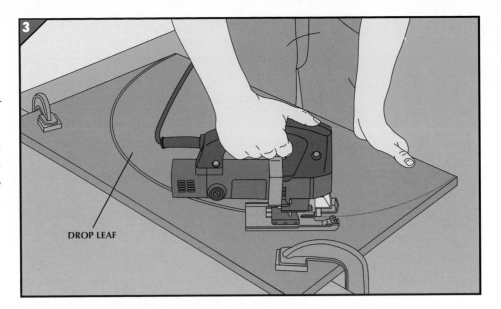

DROP LEAF

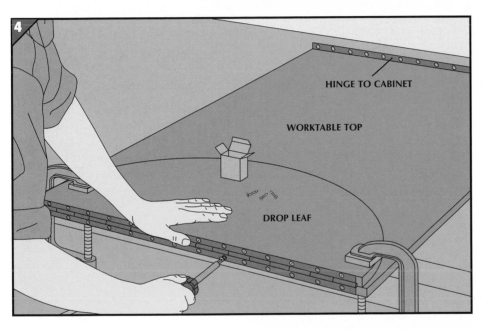

HINGE TO CABINET

WORKTABLE TOP

DROP LEAF

4. Attaching hinges to the top.

◆ Lay the worktable face-up and, with a hacksaw, cut two lengths of piano hinge slightly shorter than its width.

◆ Attach the bottom leaf of one hinge to one end of the worktable. This hinge will hold the table to the fixed shelf of the cabinet.

◆ Clamp the drop leaf to the worktable so its straight edge is flush with the table's outside end and centered between the edges.

◆ Fasten the bottom leaf of the second hinge to the edge of the worktable (left) and the top leaf to the edge of the drop leaf.

5. Making the shelf unit.

◆ For the shelf unit, cut the sides 27 inches long and the top, bottom, and shelves $21\frac{3}{4}$ inches long; make all the pieces 8 inches wide.

◆ Assemble the unit as you did the door cabinet (page 22, Step 2), joining the top and bottom to the sides with rabbets and screws, and fixing the shelf in dadoes in the sides.

◆ Tack $\frac{1}{2}$-inch plastic furniture pins to the bottom corners of the unit to serve as feet (right).

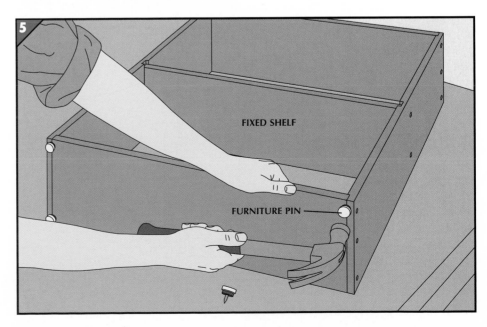

FIXED SHELF

FURNITURE PIN

MOUNTING THE ASSEMBLY

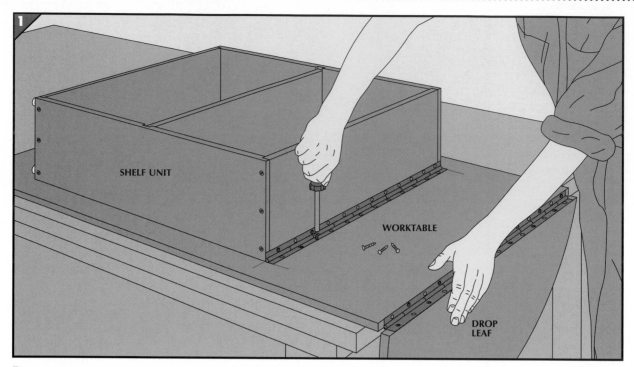

SHELF UNIT

WORKTABLE

DROP LEAF

1. Attaching the shelf unit to the table.
◆ Place the worktable face-down, then mark one line across it 12 inches from the drop leaf, and draw two intersecting lines $3\frac{1}{2}$ inches from each side.
◆ Lay the shelf unit on its back on the worktable, aligning the top corners with the intersecting marks.

◆ With a hacksaw, cut a piano hinge to the length of the shelf unit's width, then screw one leaf to the worktable *(above)* and the other to the shelf unit.
◆ Attach a commercial drop-leaf support to the underside of the worktable with the screw, nut, and washer supplied.

2. Hinging the worktable to the cabinet.
◆ Lay the door cabinet on its back, then have a helper position the table on top so the free leaf of the piano hinge is aligned along the upper half of the fixed double shelf, and the table is flush with the shelf.
◆ Screw the hinge to the shelf.
◆ Stand the unit up, extending the worktable out and the shelf unit down.
◆ Install a hydraulic arm, fastening one bracket to a cabinet side and the other to the worktable with the screws supplied *(right)*; follow the manufacturer's instructions for the exact placement of the brackets. Although most hydraulic arms will keep the table folded up securely, for added safety, install a locking hook on the outside of a cabinet side and a matching eye catch on the outer edge of the worktable *(inset)*.

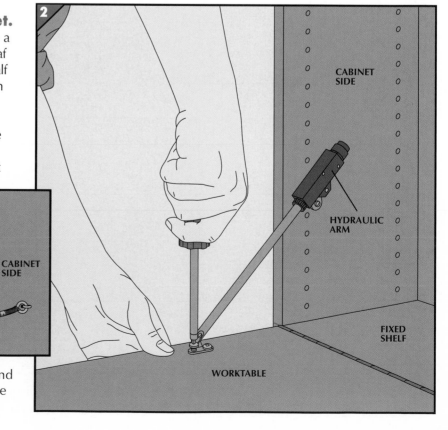

SHELF UNIT **TABLE** **CABINET SIDE**

CABINET SIDE

HYDRAULIC ARM

FIXED SHELF

WORKTABLE

HANGING THE DOOR CABINET

1. Removing the door stops.
◆ Take the closet door off its hinges. If the existing door had only two hinges, you will need to buy a third hinge for the cabinet. Unscrew the leaves from the door and the jamb, and set them aside for the door cabinet.
◆ With a mallet and a wood chisel, remove the door stops from the closet door frame *(right)*.
◆ Repaint or refinish the jamb, as needed, where the stops were removed.

DOOR STOP

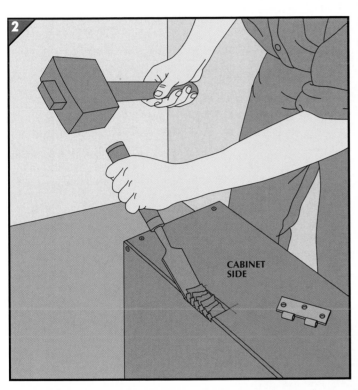

CABINET SIDE

2. Cutting hinge mortises.
◆ Mark positions for three equally spaced hinges on the jambs, then transfer the positions to the side of the cabinet, flush with the edge of the back panel that does not overhang the side. Mark the mortise depth—equal to the hinge-leaf thickness, typically $\frac{3}{16}$ inch—on the back panel.
◆ Score the mortise outlines with a utility knife and a straightedge.
◆ Cut each mortise with a chisel that has a blade width equal to the mortise width. First, hold the chisel vertically along the scored lines and tap the handle with a mallet, then make a series of cuts along the mortise, tilting the chisel *(left)*. Place the flat edge of the chisel against the depth mark on the back panel and clean out the bottom of the mortise.

3. Mounting the cabinet.
◆ Screw one leaf of each hinge into the jamb mortises and the other into the mortises in the cabinet.
◆ With two helpers, lift the door cabinet into position so the hinge leaves on the cabinet and jamb engage.
◆ With the helpers holding the cabinet steady, slip each hinge pin partially in place, starting with the bottom hinge. Drive the pins all the way in with a cold chisel and a hammer *(right)*.

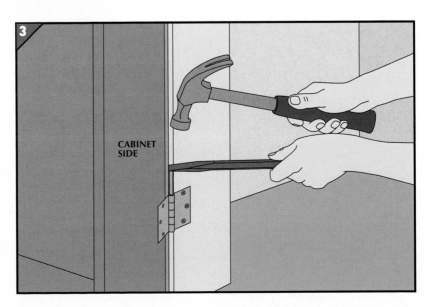

CABINET SIDE

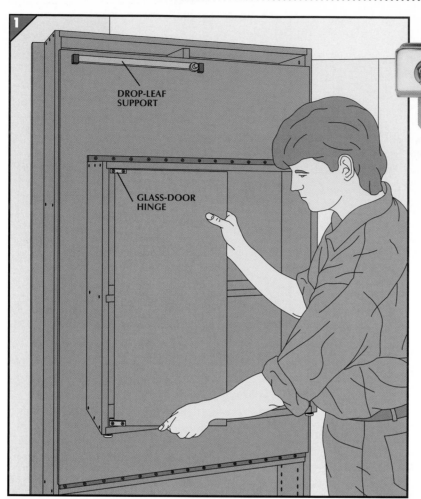

DROP-LEAF SUPPORT

GLASS-DOOR HINGE

HINGE SET PIN

1. Adding the shelf-unit doors.

◆ Cut a pair of doors from $\frac{1}{4}$-inch hardboard slightly smaller than the interior dimensions of the shelf unit.

◆ Fit an electric drill with a bit of the same diameter as the set pins of the glass-door hinges *(photograph)* you will be using—you'll need two hinges per door—and bore a hole for each pin in the top and bottom of the shelf unit. Follow the manufacturer's instructions for the exact placement of the holes.

◆ Slip the hinges into their holes, then fit one of the doors into the hinges on one side of the opening *(left)* so there is an even gap between the door and the side piece of the shelf unit. Tighten the hinge screws. Hang the second door in the same manner.

2. Mounting door latches.

◆ Slip the metal clip supplied with the glass-door hinge kit on the top of each door, flush with the outer edge.

◆ Close the doors and mark the positions of the clips on the front edge of the top of the shelf unit.

◆ Screw the magnetic latch to the underside of the top within each set of marks *(right)* so the clips will contact the latches when the doors are closed.

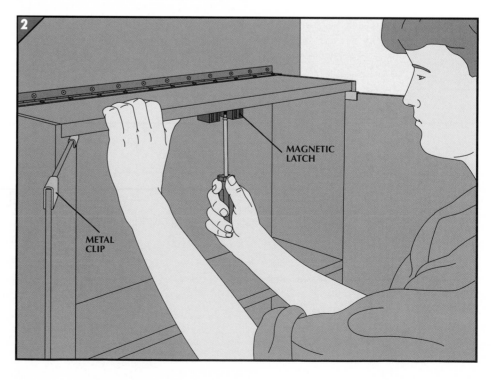

MAGNETIC LATCH

METAL CLIP

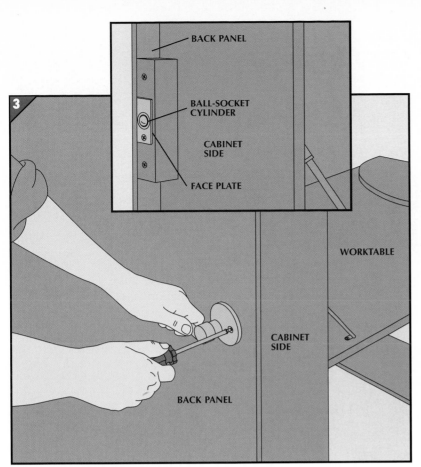

BACK PANEL

BALL-SOCKET CYLINDER

CABINET SIDE

FACE PLATE

WORKTABLE

CABINET SIDE

BACK PANEL

3. Attaching a door pull.

◆ Remove the strike plate from the door frame and replace it with the plate of a ball-socket cylinder.

◆ Cut a 2-by-2 to a length of 6 inches and a width of $1\frac{1}{4}$ inches, drill a hole into the middle of one side to accommodate the ball-socket cylinder, then screw the cylinder face plate to the piece. Screw the 2-by-2 to the side of the cabinet flush against the overhanging back panel so the cylinder engages the strike plate when the unit is closed *(inset)*.

◆ With the worktable extended, attach a door pull to the outside of the back, driving a screw into the edge of the cabinet *(left)*; use a $\frac{3}{4}$-inch bolt, washer, and nut in the other hole.

A ROLLING CABINET

When extra storage is needed for hobby supplies or tools, a practical solution is to build a cabinet that can be stowed in the closet and wheeled out next to the worktable for easy access. The unit shown here is designed much like the door cabinet, with rabbets and screws joining the top and bottom to the sides, and a back panel glued and screwed in place. A drawer *(page 13)* sits on a shelf *(page 22, Step 2)* fixed in dadoes routed in the sides. An option shown here is an overhanging false top, larger than the structural top, fastened down with screws driven from underneath. Size the parts to fit the closet, and customize the unit with drawers and shelves placed as desired. Screw plate casters *(photograph)* to the bottom corners.

A Cedar Lining

The time-honored practice of lining a closet with red cedar is a sensible idea when you need a safe place to store woolens and fine clothing. The aromatic wood keeps moths at bay without help from chemicals.

Obtaining the Wood: Tongue-and-groove red cedar is readily available at lumberyards in boards $2\frac{1}{2}$ to $4\frac{1}{2}$ inches wide and $\frac{3}{8}$ inch thick. They are sold in cartons of 42-inch lengths or in bundles comprising assorted pieces 10 inches to 8 feet long. You can apply cedar to the walls alone, but the lining will be most effective if you also cover the floor, ceiling, and inside of the door. To determine how much material you need, calculate the total area of the surfaces and add 10 percent for waste.

Installation: The boards can be put up with panel adhesive, but for a more durable installation, nail them in place. Use a technique known as blind-nailing, in which the nails are driven through each board tongue, then concealed by the grooves of the adjoining pieces. Wall boards are installed horizontally so they can be fastened to the wall studs, and ceiling boards are set perpendicular to the ceiling joists.

 TOOLS

Electronic
   stud finder
Pry bar
Screwdriver
Carpenter's level
Hammer
Nail set
Table saw
C-clamps
Electric drill and
   hole saw

 **MATERIALS**

Red-cedar boards
Wood shims
Finishing nails ($1\frac{1}{4}$")

 SAFETY TIPS

Goggles protect your eyes when you are hammering.

A cedar closet.
The closet at right is lined completely with red-cedar boards. The back, side, and front walls are covered first, then the ceiling and floor. Trim is installed around the bottom and top of the closet, the inside of the door is covered, and cedar door stops are fastened to the jambs in place of standard stops. On the walls, the boards are installed starting from the bottom with the tongues facing up, so the nails can be driven through the tongues, then concealed in the grooves of the subsequent boards. The ceiling and floor are covered in a similar manner, with the groove of the first boards flush against the starting wall.

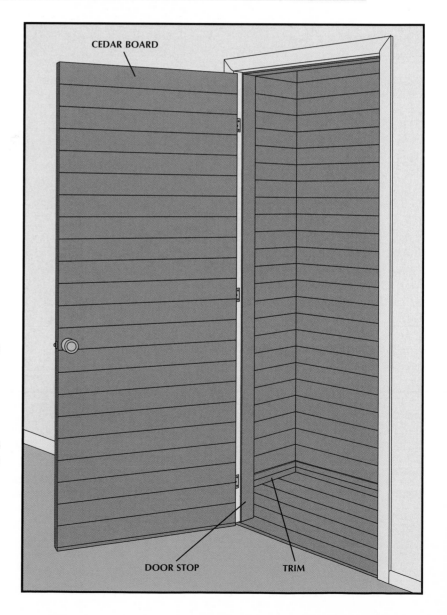

CEDAR BOARD

DOOR STOP

TRIM

1. Leveling the first board.

◆ Remove any fittings and trim from inside the closet, including closet rods and sockets, shelves and brackets, door stops, and molding.

◆ Locate and mark the studs on the closet walls, drawing locator lines from floor to ceiling.

◆ Cut a cedar board to fit along the back wall, then set it in place on the closet floor with its tongue facing up. If two or more boards are required to span the distance between the side walls, butt them end to end.

◆ Place a carpenter's level on the edge of the board near one end and slip a shim under it, if necessary, to level it. Move the level along the board to the opposite end, adding shims as needed *(right)*.

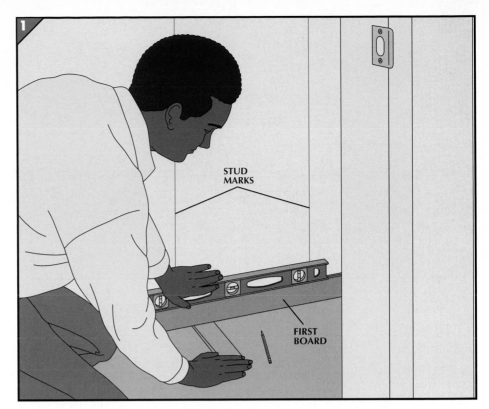

STUD MARKS

FIRST BOARD

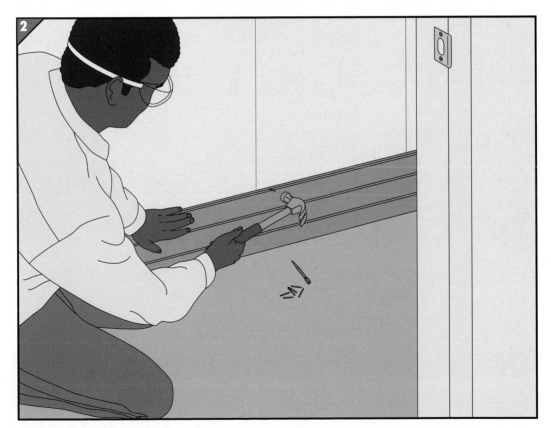

2. Covering the back wall.

◆ Drive a 1¼-inch finishing nail through the middle of the board into the wall at each stud mark. Remove the shims.

◆ Sink the nailheads with a nail set.

◆ Fit a board over the first one, inserting its groove onto the tongue of the first.

◆ Blind-nail the second board by driving a nail at a 45-degree angle through the base of the tongue into each stud. Sink the nailheads.

◆ Continue blind-nailing boards to the back wall *(above)* until you are between one and two board widths from the ceiling.

3. Fitting the last two boards.

◆ Set the next-to-last board in place, but do not nail it.

◆ Measure the gap between the board tongue and the ceiling, then trim the last board to width on a table saw, cutting off the tongue side.

◆ Pull the tongue edge of the next-to-last board slightly away from the wall and set the groove of the last piece over it.

◆ Angle the groove edge of the last board outward, then push both pieces against the wall *(left)*, closing the joint.

◆ Nail both boards in place as you did the first one.

4. Nailing the remaining boards.

◆ Install boards on the side walls in the same way you covered the back wall, butting one end of the pieces against the boards on the back wall and the other against the front wall.

◆ Cover the front walls *(right)*, cutting the boards to fit from the pieces on the side walls and end flush with the outer face of the door jambs.

◆ Line the ceiling and floor with cedar, fitting the boards snugly between the pieces fastened to the walls.

FRONT WALL

DOOR JAMB

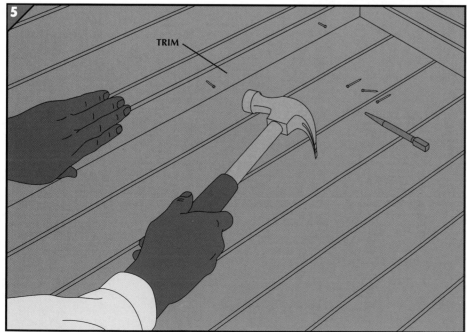

TRIM

5. Adding trim.

◆ Make trim to run along the back wall at the floor and ceiling by cutting two boards into strips $1\frac{1}{2}$ inches wide.

◆ Nail the trim to the wall, aligning the nails with those used to fasten the first and last boards.

◆ Make and fasten trim along the side *(left)* and front walls.

◆ Sink any exposed nailheads with a nail set.

6. Lining the inside of the door.

◆ Cover the inside of the door as you did the walls until you reach the doorknob, then remove the knob and measure from the center of the hole to the edge of the door and to the top edge of the last board installed below it.

◆ Transfer both measurements to the board that will cover the knob hole with crossing lines, then clamp the piece to a worktable atop a backup board, protecting the surface with wood pads.

◆ With an electric drill fitted with a $2\frac{1}{8}$-inch hole saw, center the pilot bit on the point where the marked lines intersect *(right)*, then bore a hole through the board.

◆ Nail the board in place and cover the rest of the door, then reinstall the knob.

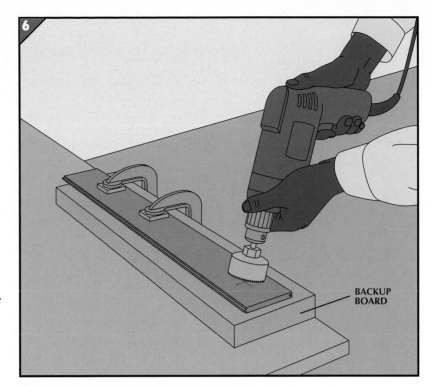

BACKUP BOARD

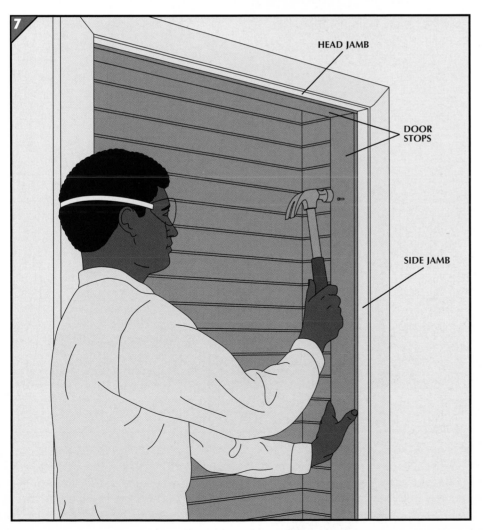

HEAD JAMB

DOOR STOPS

SIDE JAMB

7. Fastening cedar door stops.

◆ From inside the closet, close the door and mark lines on both side jambs and on the head jamb along the inside face of the door.

◆ Cut a board to fit along the head jamb between the side jambs, and trim it to width to cover the jamb between the inner face of the cedar board installed above the door opening and the marked line on the jamb.

◆ Nail the board to the head jamb, its outer edge flush with the marked line.

◆ For each side jamb, cut a board to fit between the head jamb and the floor, trimming it to cover the jamb between the marked line on the jamb and the inner face of the cedar boards on the front walls of the closet.

◆ Fasten the boards to the jambs *(left)*.

When a house lacks sufficient closet space, one solution is to add a closet by enclosing a corner of a room with two partition walls.

Getting Started: The closet's size will be partially dependent on the available space in the room, but plan it to be at least 27 inches deep and, if possible, size it so its walls can be anchored to studs behind the existing walls; otherwise, add nailer blocks behind the wallboard for support *(page 36)*.

Buy the doors before building the walls so that you can frame the opening to the correct dimensions. Remove shoe molding and baseboards from the area before you begin. You can reinstall them once construction is completed, and add matching trim along the exterior of the closet.

Doors: Bifold doors are available with louvered or solid panels hinged together in pairs. Generally, one

pair of panels is mounted at each side of the opening to fold back against the sides or pull in toward the center *(pages 41-43)*. Another method of installation is to mount all the panels on one side so that they fold against that side or pull across the opening.

> **⚠ CAUTION** *If you will be cutting into walls, check first for the presence of lead and asbestos* (page 45).

 TOOLS

Electronic stud finder
Chalk line
Carpenter's square
Plumb bob
Circular saw
Hammer
Combination square
Carpenter's level
Backsaw

Utility knife
Caulking gun
Pry bar
Electric drill
Clutch-driven
  screwdriver bit
Tin snips
Taping knives
  (5", 8", 10")
Hacksaw
Screwdriver

 MATERIALS

1 x 3s, 2 x 4s
Cedar shims
Common nails
  (3", $3\frac{1}{2}$")
Wallboard screws
  ($1\frac{1}{2}$")
Ring-shank wall-
  board nails ($1\frac{1}{2}$")
Wallboard ($\frac{1}{2}$")

Wallboard adhesive
Corner bead
Joint compound
Joint tape
  (pre-creased paper
  and fiberglass)
Sandpaper
  (medium grade)
Bifold doors and
  installation kit

 SAFETY TIPS

Wear goggles when operating power tools and hammering, and a dust mask when sanding joint compound.

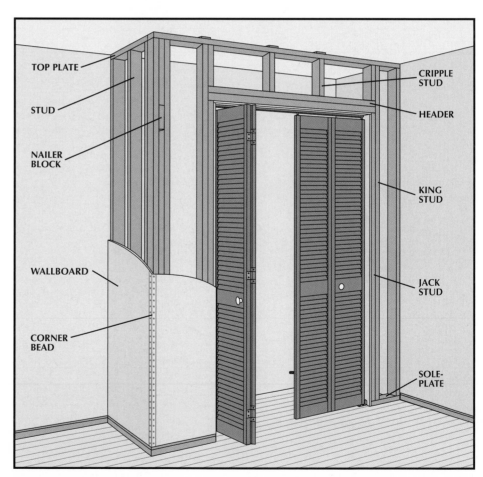

Anatomy of a closet.
The closet above is made of two partition walls with studs spaced at 16-inch intervals between top plates and soleplates, and an extra stud and nailer blocks at the corner. At the ends, the partitions are anchored to studs or nailer blocks behind the existing walls *(page 36)*. The doorway is framed with jack and king studs at the sides, and a header and cripple studs at the top. Wallboard covers the framing inside and outside, and bifold doors are installed in the opening.

FRAMING THE WALLS

STUD MARK

1. Laying out the walls.
◆ With a stud finder, locate the studs on each side of the corner where the closet will be located. Mark the locations at the top and bottom of the wall.
◆ Draw the outline of the interior of the closet on the ceiling, using a carpenter's square to make 90-degree corners.
◆ Have a helper drop a plumb bob from the ceiling at the outlined corner of the partition walls. Mark the point indicated on the floor *(left)*, then outline the interior of the closet on the floor.

2. Assembling the walls.
◆ Measure and cut two 2-by-4s to length to serve as the top plate and soleplate for each partition wall, planning for the front wall to overlap the end wall at the outside corner.
◆ Lay each wall's top plate and soleplate side by side and mark $1\frac{1}{2}$-inch-wide stud locations on them with a combination square. Start with a stud at one end and space the stud centers at 16-inch intervals—except at the doorway—finishing with a stud at the other end.
◆ Mark locations for adjoining jack and king studs on each side of the doorway at the distance specified by the door manufacturer—allow for an extra $\frac{1}{2}$ inch on each side to account for the thickness of the wallboard you will use to finish the opening.
◆ Measure from the ceiling to the floor at three points along the closet's marked outline and cut 2-by-4 studs $3\frac{1}{4}$ inches shorter than the smallest measurement—to allow for the combined thickness of the plates and for

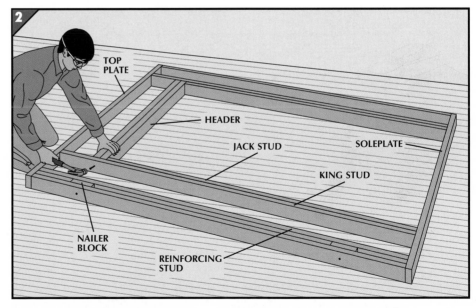

TOP PLATE
HEADER
JACK STUD
SOLEPLATE
KING STUD
NAILER BLOCK
REINFORCING STUD

clearance when raising the walls.
◆ Set the plates on edge and fasten the studs to them, driving two $3\frac{1}{2}$-inch common nails through each plate into the end of the stud.
◆ Cut two 3-inch-long 1-by-4 nailer blocks, place them against the stud at the end of the front wall that will overlap the end wall, and nail a reinforcing stud to them and to the plates.
◆ Frame the doorway with full-height

king studs and jack studs $\frac{1}{4}$ inch shorter than the height of the door units fastened together with 3-inch nails, then nail a header made of two 2-by-4s in place at the top of the opening on the ends of the jack studs and between the king studs *(above)*.
◆ Cut cripple studs to fit between the header and the top plate, then nail them in place on 16-inch centers and at each end of the header.

3. Raising the walls.

◆ If either partition wall falls between studs, cut slots in the wallboard and install nailer blocks *(inset)* about one-third and two-thirds of the way up the wall. Patch the slots with wallboard *(pages 37-38).*

◆ With a helper, tilt the end wall upright and into place.

◆ While the helper holds the frame and checks for plumb with a carpenter's level, push pairs of tapered wood shims into each side of the gap between the end stud and existing wall where you will nail into a stud or nailer block and between the top plate and the ceiling where you will nail into a joist.

◆ Drive nails partway through the end stud and shims into the stud or nailer block *(right).*

◆ Raise the front wall into place in the same way.

NAILER BLOCK

4. Anchoring the walls.

◆ Once both walls are positioned and plumb, secure them at the outside corner by driving two nails at an angle through the end of the front wall and three nails through the end of the side wall into the front corner.

◆ Nail the top plate and shims to the joists *(left)* and finish driving the nails into the studs.

◆ Score the protruding shims with a utility knife and snap them off.

5. Completing the door opening.
◆ Protecting the floor with cardboard, cut away the soleplate from the door opening with a backsaw *(left)*.
◆ Nail the soleplates at intervals of 16 inches to floor joists, where possible, or to the flooring.

PUTTING UP WALLBOARD

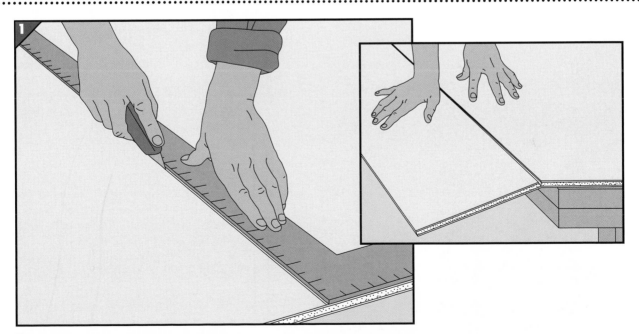

1. Scoring and snapping a panel.
◆ Measure and mark the panel to size, then lay a carpenter's square at the mark and score the paper with a utility knife *(above)*.
◆ Place support blocks under the panel along the good side of the cut, then press down sharply on the waste side, breaking the wallboard along the cut *(inset)*.
◆ Cock the waste section up slightly, then reach behind the panel with the knife and slit the paper along the bend.
◆ Snap the waste piece down to break it off.

2. Fastening the wallboard.

◆ Mark the stud positions on the ceiling and the floor for reference.

◆ With a caulking gun, apply a $\frac{3}{8}$-inch-thick zigzag bead of wallboard adhesive to each stud the panel will cover, starting and stopping about 6 inches from where the edges will fall.

◆ Fit an electric drill with a clutch-driven screwdriver bit—also called a dimpler—which automatically stops screws at the correct depth.

◆ Lift the panel into place against the ceiling, using a pry bar on a scrap of wood as a lever.

◆ Fasten the panel to each stud with $1\frac{1}{2}$-inch wallboard screws spaced about 2 feet apart, starting 1 inch from the top and stopping 1 inch from the bottom (right).

◆ At outside corners—including those at the sides and top of the doorway—lap the end of the second piece over the first and screw into the common stud or the header. At an inside corner, butt one panel against the other and fasten only the second piece to a stud or the header. Where two sheets meet on the outside or inside of the front wall, cut them to fall at the center of a stud and fasten each edge to the stud.

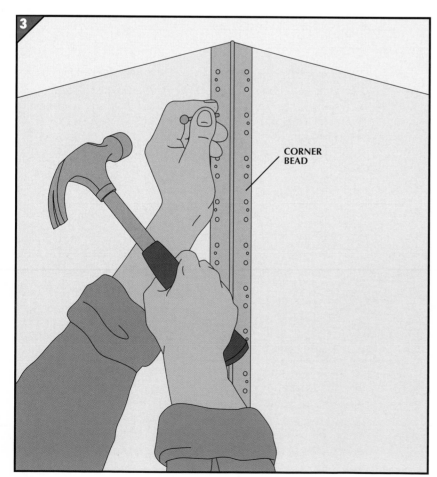

CORNER BEAD

3. Adding corner bead.

◆ For each outside corner of wallboard, including those at the sides and top of the doorway, trim a strip of metal corner bead to the correct length with tin snips, cutting through one flange at a time.

◆ Position the corner bead over the joint and drive $1\frac{1}{2}$-inch ring-shank wallboard nails through its holes into the stud (left).

◆ Load the left two-thirds of a 5-inch taping knife with joint compound.

◆ With the right 2 inches of the blade overhanging the corner, draw the knife smoothly down the left side of the corner bead.

◆ Load the right side of the knife and run it down the right side of the bead.

◆ Scrape the knife clean, then remove excess compound and smooth the joint by drawing the blade alternately down the bead's left and right faces, then let the compound dry.

◆ Apply and smooth a second coat of compound without letting the knife overhang the corner, feathering this layer about $1\frac{1}{2}$ inches beyond the first.

4. Covering screwheads.

◆ Load half the width of the taping knife with joint compound.

◆ Holding the blade almost parallel to the wallboard, draw the knife across the screwhead, filling the dimple completely with compound *(right)*.

◆ Raise the blade of the knife to a more upright position and scrape off excess compound with a single stroke at right angles to the first.

◆ Let the compound dry, then apply one more coat in the same way.

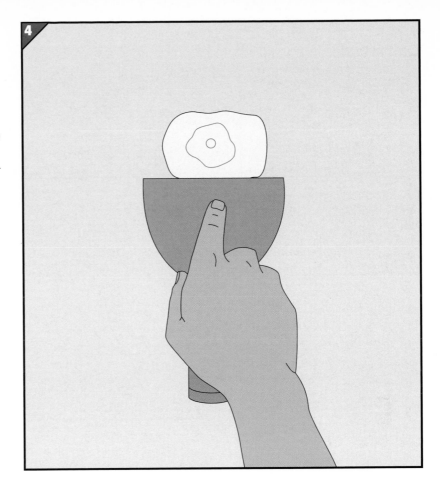

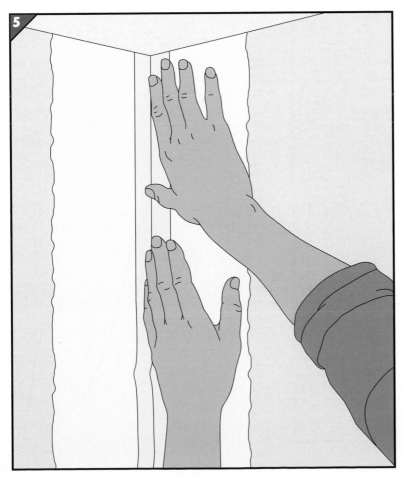

5. Taping inside corners.

◆ Load half the width of the knife with joint compound.

◆ Run the knife along one side of the corner joint and then the other, lifting the inside edge of the blade slightly to provide a thicker layer of compound at the joint. (Some compound may get scraped off the first side while coating the second, but this will not affect the result.)

◆ Fold paper joint tape along its lengthwise crease and press it lightly into the joint compound with your fingers *(left)*.

◆ Run the knife along both sides of the crease, applying just enough force for the tape to stick to the compound.

◆ Make a second pass, apply greater pressure on the knife to smooth the tape and squeeze out excess compound.

◆ Coat the tape lightly with some of the excess compound, then make a third pass, leaving a film of compound on the tape.

6. Taping flat seams.

◆ Press the end of a roll of self-adhesive fiberglass-mesh joint tape to the wall at one end of the joint.

◆ Unwind the tape with one hand and press it into the joint with your hand or with the taping knife. If the tape wrinkles, lift it, pull it tight, and press it into place.

◆ Cut the tape off the roll when you reach the end of the joint.

◆ Load the knife with joint compound and cover the tape with a thin layer of compound *(right)*.

◆ Make a second pass along the joint, pressing firmly to smooth the compound and scrape off the excess.

◆ Make a third pass with the knife to eliminate any air bubbles.

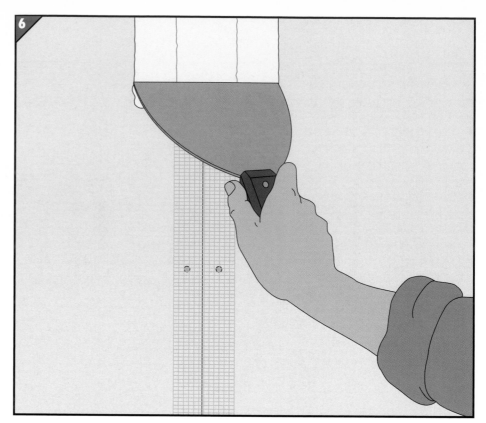

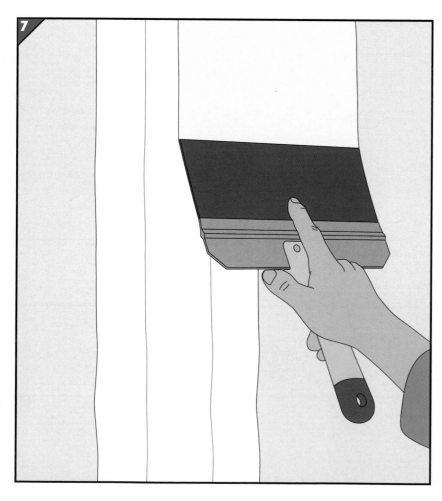

7. Feathering the compound.

Make a final application of compound, feathering the edges to create a smooth, uniform surface.

◆ With an 8-inch knife, apply compound at outside corners and feather it an additional 2 inches on each side of the corner bead.

◆ Cover screwheads with compound and feather the edges outward by 2 inches.

◆ At inside corners, apply compound on one side of the joint and then the other, feathering the edges by 2 inches on each surface.

◆ Apply compound to a flat seam with a 10-inch knife, then draw the blade along each side of the joint, lifting the edge nearest the joint about $\frac{1}{8}$ inch to create a slight ridge that feathers out evenly on both sides *(left)*.

◆ Once the final coat of compound dries, lightly smooth the surface with medium-grade sandpaper or a damp wallboard sponge.

1. Mounting the track.
◆ Trim the track with a hacksaw, if necessary, so it is $\frac{1}{8}$ inch shorter than the top of the opening.
◆ Center the track at the top of the opening and mark the screw holes.
◆ Drill pilot holes for the screws provided in the kit.
◆ Reposition the track and drive in the screws *(left)*.

2. Placing the bottom brackets.
◆ At one end of the opening, drop a plumb line from the center of the pivot bracket on the track and make a mark where it touches the floor.
◆ Set a bottom pivot bracket against the side wall of the opening, with the sides of the notched slot centered over the mark on the floor.
◆ Mark the bracket screw holes on the wall and the floor, then drill pilot holes for the screws supplied. Reposition the bracket and drive in the screws *(right)*.
◆ Install a bottom pivot bracket on the opposite side of the opening following the same procedure.

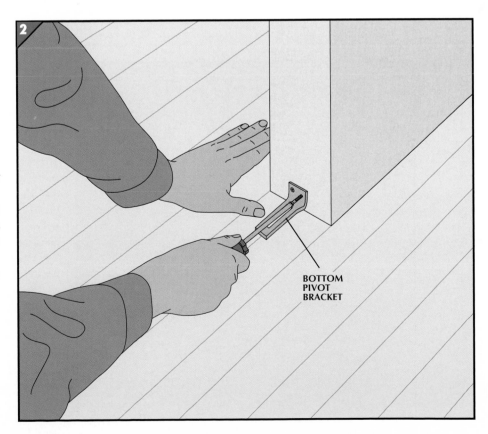

TRACK

BOTTOM PIVOT BRACKET

3. Preparing the doors.

◆ With a hammer, gently tap the bottom pivot into the hole at the bottom of the door panel nearest the wall, then seat another pivot in the hole at the top of the panel. Fit the third pivot into the hole at the top of the other door panel.

◆ Fold the door and slip the top pivot into its bracket near the wall. Push the door upward to compress the pivot *(right)*, then insert the bottom pivot into its bracket on the floor *(inset)*.

◆ To fit the door's center pivot in the track, unfold the panels and align the track's slide guide with the pivot. Press down on the pivot and position it between the guide's two springs, then release it.

◆ Install the other door the same way.

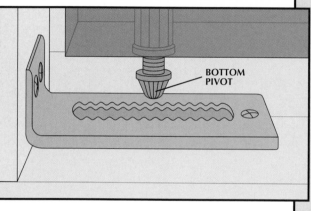

BOTTOM
PIVOT

BOTTOM
PIVOT

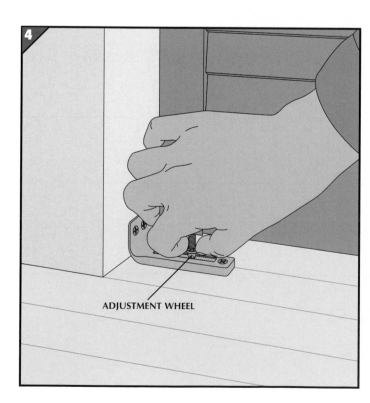

ADJUSTMENT WHEEL

4. Making door adjustments.

◆ To raise or lower a door slightly, note which notch the bottom pivot occupies in its bracket. Then, lift out the pivot and turn the adjustment wheel *(left)*: counterclockwise to lower the door, or clockwise to raise it. Reseat the pivot in the correct notch.

◆ For a lateral adjustment, lift the bottom pivot and move it to another notch. To shift the top of the door, remove the door, then loosen the screw holding the top pivot bracket and move the bracket. Retighten the screw and reinstall the door.

Once the doors are aligned, attach the door pulls.

5. Mounting the aligners.

◆ To keep the doors flush with each other when shut, close them and mount an aligner on the back of each one about 1 foot from the floor *(right)*.

◆ To fine-tune the position of each aligner, loosen the screws and slide the device along the slots until the doors close tightly together.

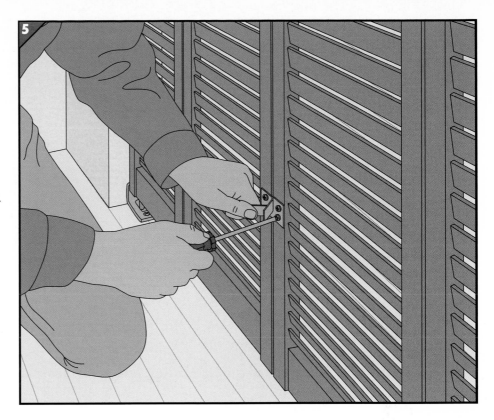

SLIDE GUIDES

6. Adding a door stop.

Drive a screw partway into the top track at the center of the opening to act as a stop for the two slide guides *(left)*.

A Kneewall Cabinet

The inaccessible space behind knee-walls—the short, vertical walls below the sloping ceiling of an attic room—can be reclaimed by converting it into closets that can be used for almost any type of storage.

Varying the Size: You can build kneewall closets to any height; however, limiting them to the height of the original wall—generally about 3 feet—will keep them from encroaching on floor space in the room. The closet on these pages is a small corner unit next to a dormer, but you can apply the same techniques to create one on any kneewall. For a room with no dormer, omit the side paneling and build the cabinet face *(page 47)* with vertical members at both ends.

TOOLS

Electronic stud finder
Carpenter's square
Utility knife
Backsaw
Hammer
Circular saw
Electric drill
Screwdriver bit

Staple gun
Wallboard tools
T-bevel
Router
Bar clamps
Saber saw
Table saw
Nail set

SAFETY TIPS

Wear gloves and a dust mask when handling fiberglass insulation and goggles when you are hammering nails or operating a power tool.

MATERIALS

Furniture-grade plywood ($\frac{3}{4}$")
Plywood ($\frac{5}{8}$")
1 x 2s, 2 x 4s
Common nails (3")
Finishing nails ($1\frac{1}{2}$")
Wood screws ($\frac{5}{8}$", $1\frac{1}{4}$", $1\frac{1}{2}$" No. 8)
Toggle bolts (2")
Fiberglass insulation
Wallboard materials
Wood glue
Semiconcealed hinges
Edge banding

Anatomy of a kneewall closet.
The closet at right is somewhat similar to a cabinet—its doors are hung on a face frame—but the cabinet frame is fastened to the wall studs. A decorative plywood panel covers the wallboard on the dormer side, and the unit is trimmed with molding and a top ledge. The closet has a plywood floor, and wallboard covers the rafters and studs inside.

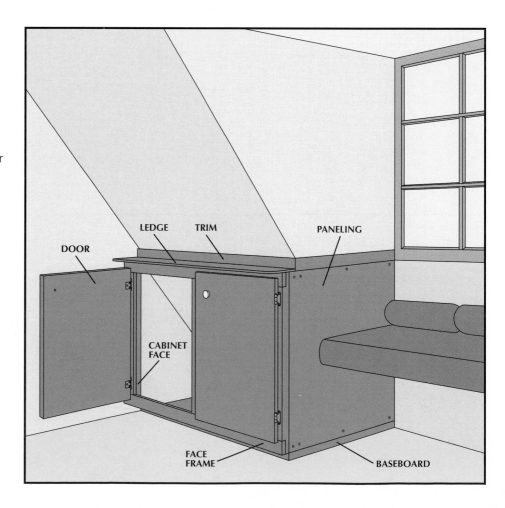

LEDGE TRIM PANELING

DOOR

CABINET FACE

FACE FRAME BASEBOARD

PREPARING THE OPENING

1. Cutting the opening.

◆ With a stud finder, locate and mark the studs behind the kneewall, then draw a horizontal line 4 inches below the junction point of the ceiling and the kneewall.

◆ Cut through the wallboard along the marked lines with a utility knife, using a carpenter's square as a guide *(right)*, then pull it away from the studs.

◆ If there are wall studs within the opening, cut them flush with the wallboard at the top, then fasten a 2-by-4 with 3-inch common nails to the cut studs and to the end studs to form a header that spans the opening.

STUD MARK

⚠ CAUTION

Safety Procedures for Lead Paint and Asbestos

Before 1978, lead was used in paint, while asbestos was found in wallboard, joint compound, and insulation. Before cutting into walls, mist the area with a solution of 1 teaspoon of low-sudsing detergent per quart of water, then cut out a small sample with a hand tool. Use a home test kit to check for lead; for asbestos, take samples to a certified lab. If either substance is present, you may want to hire a professional for the job; if you do the work yourself, follow these procedures:

❗ *Keep people and pets out of the work area.*

❗ *Wear protective clothing (available from a safety equipment store) and a dual-cartridge respirator with high-efficiency particulate air (HEPA) filters. Remove the clothing before leaving the work area, wash the items separately, and shower immediately.*

❗ *Indoors, seal off work-area openings, including windows, doors, vents, and air conditioners, with 6-mil polyethylene sheeting and duct tape. Cover nonremovable items with sheeting and tape, and turn off forced-air heating and cooling systems.*

❗ *Never sand or cut material with power tools— mist them with detergent and remove them with a hand tool.*

❗ *Mop the area twice when the job is done. Place all debris in a 6-mil polyethylene bag and call your health department or environmental protection agency for disposal guidelines.*

2. Laying a subfloor.

◆ Cut a piece of $\frac{5}{8}$-inch plywood to run the length of the closet and fit between the rafters and the soleplate at the bottom of the kneewall.

◆ Lay the subfloor in place and fasten it to the joists with $1\frac{1}{4}$-inch No. 8 wood screws driven every 6 inches *(right)*.

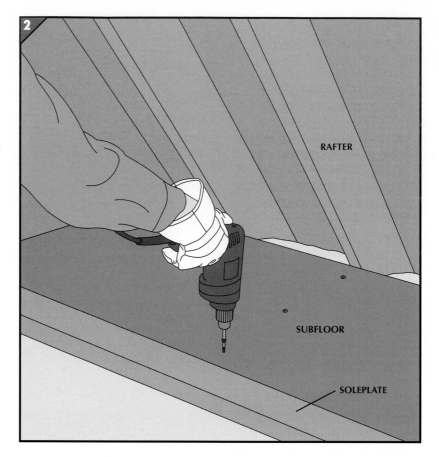

3. Covering the inside walls.

◆ Staple insulation—vapor barrier facing inside—to the rafters inside the closet, then cover the rafters with wallboard *(pages 37-40)*.

◆ If there are no studs on the end walls, make a nailer to support the wallboard: With a T-bevel, find the angle of the rafters, then miter one end of a 2-by-4 at that angle. Choose a location for the new stud—roughly halfway along the side wall—and cut the board to fit there between the floor and the ceiling.

◆ Position the nailer against the end wall and fasten it to the subfloor and the rafter behind the wallboard with $1\frac{1}{2}$-inch screws *(left)*.

◆ Cover the side walls with wallboard.

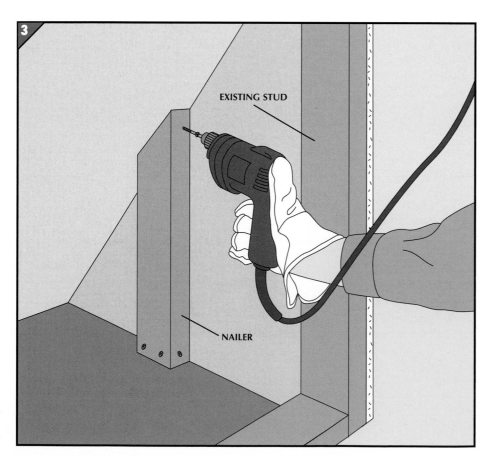

BUILDING THE UNIT

1. Assembling the cabinet face.

◆ Toenail a new stud to the header and soleplate in the center of the opening.

◆ Make cleats from short pieces of 1-by-2 and screw one to the front of the header on each side of the center stud and $\frac{3}{4}$ inch from each end.

◆ Build a cabinet face from strips of $\frac{3}{4}$-inch plywood cut 4 inches wide. Cut a vertical end piece to reach from a point $2\frac{1}{4}$ inches above the floor to the top of the header and two horizontal strips to span from the inner face of the vertical piece to the opposite end of the opening. Add a second vertical piece to fit between the horizontal strips. Fasten the pieces together with two $1\frac{1}{4}$-inch screws per joint, positioning the second vertical piece so it will be centered over the middle stud.

◆ Set the assembly on the cleats and fasten it to them with screws. Drill holes to accommodate 2-inch toggle bolts in the end strip *(left)*, then bolt it to the wall.

◆ Cut a plywood panel the same height as the cabinet face to cover the outside end wall. Attach it to the wall studs and cabinet face with countersunk screws.

2. Adding the face frame.

◆ Cut four 1-by-2s to form a frame that will sit flush with the outer sides of the cabinet face and the paneling.

◆ Cut a rabbet *(page 10)* across each end of the pieces, making repeated passes half as deep as the thickness of the stock across the full width of the pieces, to form joints known as half laps *(inset)*.

◆ Spread wood glue in all the rabbets and assemble the pieces, setting them on wood blocks.

◆ Check with a carpenter's square that the corners form 90-degree angles, then secure the pieces with small bar clamps *(right)*.

◆ When the glue is dry, remove the clamps and attach the face frame to the edges of the cabinet face with $\frac{5}{8}$-inch No. 8 screws driven at each corner and at 8-inch intervals in between.

◆ Cut a 1-by-2 to fit between the horizontal pieces of the frame and screw it to the center strip of the cabinet face.

◆ Apply edge banding to any visible plywood edges *(page 12)*.

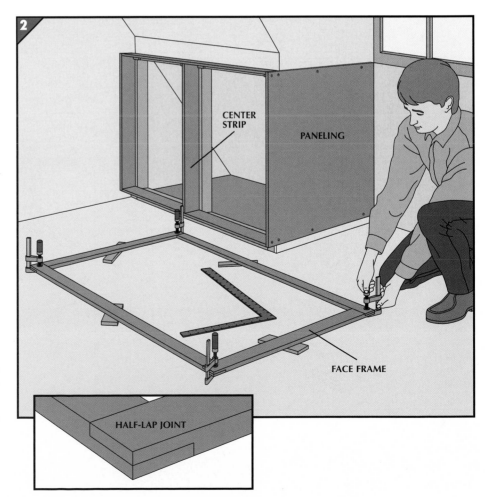

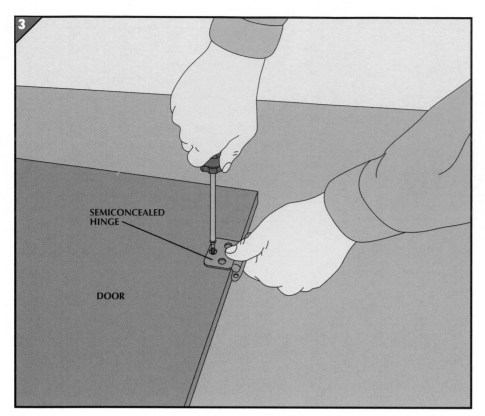

3. Attaching the door hinges.
◆ From $\frac{3}{4}$-inch plywood, cut a pair of doors 1 inch larger all around than the openings in the face frame.
◆ Apply edge banding to the door edges *(page 12)*.
◆ Mark hinge positions on one edge of each door one-quarter of the way from the top and bottom.
◆ At each marked location, position a hinge suitable for face frames—such as the semiconcealed hinge shown here—and fasten it to the door *(left)*.

INVISIBLE EUROPEAN HINGES

If you prefer hinges that are hidden, consider installing European-style hardware. For the kneewall cabinets on these pages, buy hinges intended to be attached to face frames *(right)* rather than those made for frameless cabinets. Since the hinges must be mounted in precisely located holes on the doors, use a special jig made for the purpose. The jig has a guide fence on its underside and a pair of swivel stops that situate each hole correctly in relation to the ends and edges of the door. A 35-mm Forstner bit in an electric drill mounts to the underside of the jig and is stopped at the correct depth automatically.

To attach the hinges, use the jig to drill a hole for the body of each hinge on the door's inner face near the top and bottom. Separate each hinge into its parts and fasten the boss to the door. Reassemble the hinges and position the door on the unit so that the hinge plates sit on the inner edge of the face frame. Mark the screw holes, take the hinges apart again, and fasten the plates to the unit, then hang the door.

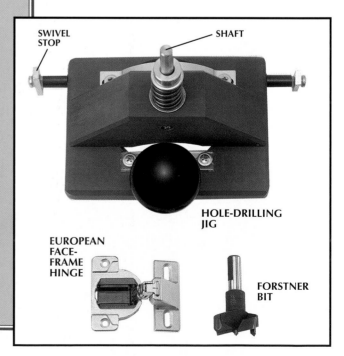

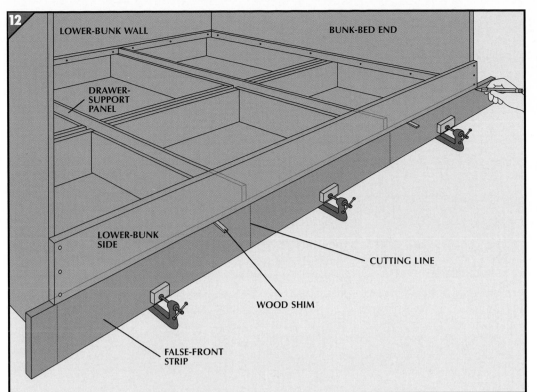

LOWER-BUNK WALL

BUNK-BED END

DRAWER-SUPPORT PANEL

LOWER-BUNK SIDE

CUTTING LINE

WOOD SHIM

FALSE-FRONT STRIP

12. Adding drawer false fronts.

◆ With the drawers in place, secure the two false-front strips *(Step 1)* across them with C-clamps, placing wood shims between the strips and the lower-bunk side to maintain a $\frac{1}{16}$-inch gap between pieces; protect the surfaces of the strips with wood pads.

◆ Mark cutting lines across the strips at the midpoint of the drawer-support panels and $\frac{1}{16}$ inch in from the outer edges of the bunk-bed ends *(left)*, so the drawers will clear the bookshelf-closet section after the final assembly is completed.

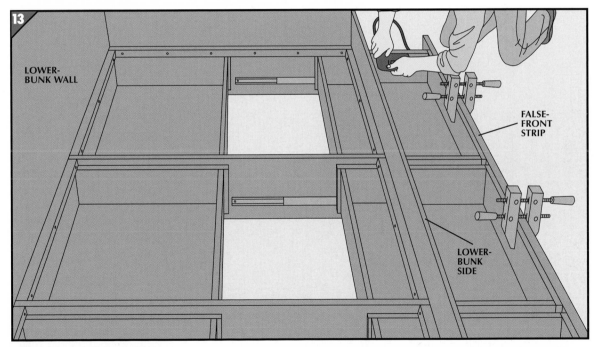

LOWER-BUNK WALL

FALSE-FRONT STRIP

LOWER-BUNK SIDE

13. The final assembly.

◆ Pull the three drawers on one side of the bed/divider open simultaneously, taking care not to disturb the false-front strip clamped across them.

◆ Leaving the C-clamps in place, hold the top edge of the strip in place with three handscrew clamps.

◆ At each corner of the drawer fronts, drill a pilot hole for a $1\frac{1}{4}$-inch screw through the drawer into the false-front strip *(above)*; the holes will help you reposition the strip after cutting it into sections.

◆ Unclamp the strip and cut it along the lines made in Step 12.

◆ Align the pilot holes in each drawer front with those in its false front and screw the pieces together.

◆ Attach drawer pulls *(page 64, Step 5)*, then repeat the process to attach the false fronts on the drawers on the opposite side.

MAKING THE BOOKCASE-CLOSET AND CABINET

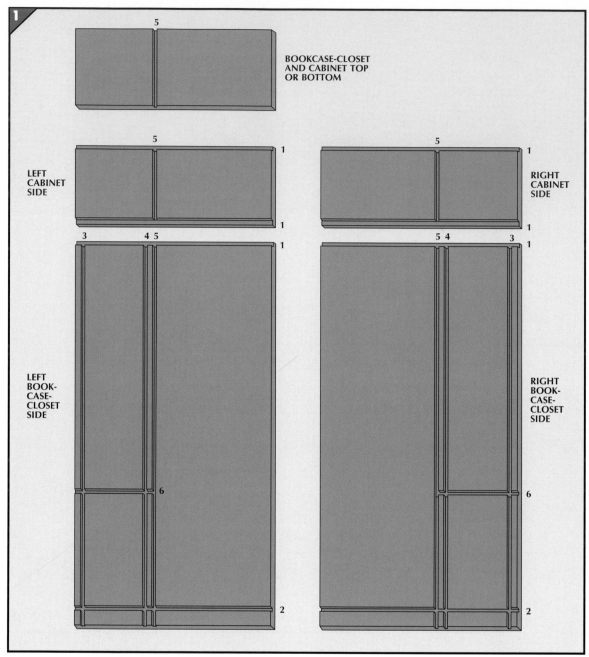

BOOKCASE-CLOSET AND CABINET TOP OR BOTTOM

LEFT CABINET SIDE

RIGHT CABINET SIDE

LEFT BOOK-CASE-CLOSET SIDE

RIGHT BOOK-CASE-CLOSET SIDE

1. Planning the joinery.
The illustrations above show the rabbets and dadoes *(pages 10-11)* required to join the parts of the bookcase-closet and the cabinet. Saw the sides, tops, and bottom to size, then outline and label the cuts on the inner faces of the pieces as follows: Cut rabbets at the top of the bookcase-closet sides and at the top and bottom of the

cabinet sides *(1)* $\frac{3}{4}$ inch wide and $\frac{1}{4}$ inch deep. Make the dadoes that hold the bottom panel of the bookcase and closet *(2)* the same size, and locate them 3 inches from the bottoms of the sides. For shelf standards *(page 21)* in the bookcase, size the dadoes according to the width and depth of the hardware, and place them $1\frac{3}{8}$ inches *(3)* and $14\frac{5}{8}$ inches *(4)* from

the front edges. Rout dadoes $\frac{3}{8}$ inch wide and $\frac{3}{16}$ inch deep $16\frac{5}{8}$ inches from the front edges *(5)* for the back panels in the bookcase-closet sides, top, and bottom, as well as for the partition in the cabinet sides, tops, and bottom. Cut the dadoes for the fixed shelf in the sides of the bookcase *(6)* $\frac{3}{4}$ inch wide, $\frac{1}{4}$ inch deep, and $27\frac{1}{4}$ inches from the bottom.

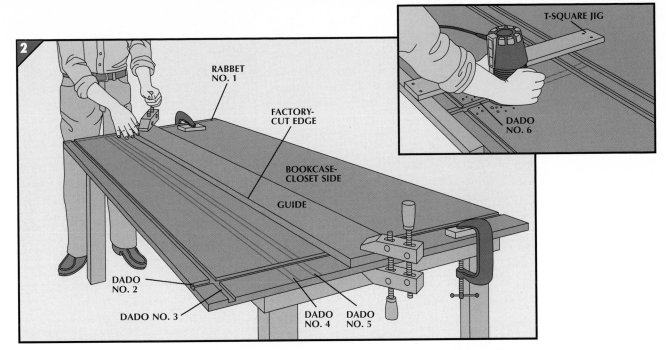

2. Making the cuts.

◆ Clamp a bookshelf-closet side inside-face up to a worktable, protecting the surface with wood pads, and cut rabbet No. 1 along the top in a similar manner to the one on page 10.

◆ To make dadoes No. 2, No. 3, No. 4, and No. 5, use a piece of plywood the length of the side with the factory-cut edge facing the dado as a router guide in the same manner as described on page 11. Reposition the guide before you cut each dado, clamping it to the workpiece *(above)*.

◆ For dado No. 6, make a T-square jig to help position the cut. Size the leg of the jig at least 18 inches long plus the width of the crosspiece and place it against the side of the workpiece to make the cut *(inset)*.

3. Attaching the desk drop leaves to the fixed shelves.

◆ Cut the two fixed shelves and drop leaves to size, making the drop leaf $1\frac{1}{2}$ inches wider than the shelf. Set each pair face-down and end-to-end on a worktable so the edges of the drop leaf extend beyond those of the shelf by the same amount on both sides.

◆ To keep each drop leaf level and hold the braces *(Step 4)* in position when the desk is raised, cut two plywood blocks—each $\frac{3}{4}$ inch wide and 3 inches long, with a notch at one end measuring $\frac{1}{2}$- by $\frac{3}{4}$-inch—and drill a

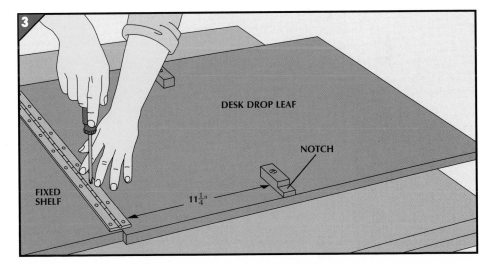

clearance hole for a $1\frac{1}{4}$-inch screw through the unnotched part of the block so it can be swiveled aside when the drop leaf is down. Attach the blocks to the underside of the drop leaf $11\frac{1}{4}$ inches from the piano hinge to be mounted.

◆ With a hacksaw, cut a length of piano hinge $\frac{1}{2}$ inch shorter than the width of the shelf, then center the hinge over the seam between the two parts, make starter holes with an awl, and fasten it in place with $\frac{5}{8}$-inch wood screws *(above)*.

4. Shelf standards and desk braces.

◆ Lay each bookshelf-closet side on a worktable, then fasten lengths of shelf standard in their dadoes on each side of the fixed-shelf dado *(page 59, Step 1)*.

◆ Make the two desk braces out of a $12\frac{1}{4}$- by $12\frac{3}{4}$-inch piece of plywood, cutting across the piece at an angle between points $1\frac{7}{8}$ inches from opposite corners on the longer sides. Clamp a scrap board under the side to support each brace in the open position, then butt the longer straight side of the brace against the bookcase-closet side $\frac{1}{4}$ inch below the fixed-shelf dado.

◆ Cut a length of piano hinge a little shorter than the seam between the brace and the side, and position it with its pin loops aligned on the edge of the bookcase-closet side.

◆ Fasten the hinge in place *(Step 3)*, then install the remaining ones in the same way, as shown at left.

◆ Fold the braces back against the bookshelf-closet sides and use masking tape to hold them there until the assembly is completed.

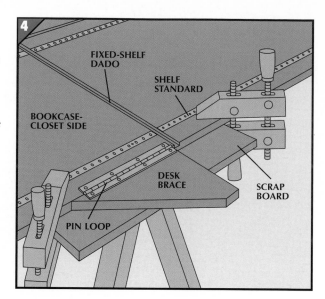

5. Assembling the bookcase-closets.

◆ Cut 3- by 3-inch base-plate notches in the bottom corners of the bookcase-closet sides, as you did for the bunkbed ends *(page 77, Step 1)*.

◆ Spread wood glue in the rabbets and dadoes of the side pieces and on the contacting edges of the pieces to be joined to them, then fit the pieces as shown at right: the bottom, back panel, fixed shelf, and top in one side piece, then the opposite side piece.

◆ Secure the assembly with two bar clamps *(page 60, Step 2)*, then drill pilot holes for $1\frac{1}{2}$-inch countersunk screws and washers through the sides into the bottom, back, shelf, and top 1 inch from the ends of the pieces and every 6 inches in between.

◆ Drive the screws, then cut and attach base plates *(page 81, Step 9)* to the cabinet sides.

◆ Cut doors to fit flush with the sides of the closet and cabinet, and attach them with European hinges similar to the ones on page 48, but designed for frameless cabinets.

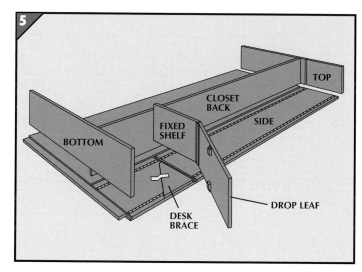

Drill holes in the doors using the techniques on page 48, but attach the hinge plates to the inside surface of the panels rather than to a face frame.

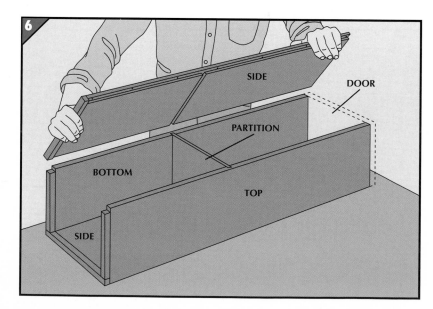

6. Building the cabinets.

◆ Cut the two partitions to fit in the dadoes dividing the top and bottom panels of the cabinets, then apply wood glue to the pieces as you did for the closet-bookcase *(Step 5)*.

◆ For each unit, place a side piece face-down on the worktable and fit the partition, top, bottom, and opposite side *(left)*.

◆ Clamp and screw the parts together, then add a door to each cabinet, as indicated by the dashed lines in the illustration.

◆ Apply edge banding *(page 12)* to all exposed edges of plywood, fasten handles and magnetic catches to the doors, and attach pulls to the drawers *(page 64, Step 5)*.

BUILDING THE LADDER

1. Routing the uprights.

◆ Cut two 1-by-6s 5 feet long for the uprights and four 1-by-4s to a length of 18 inches for the treads.

◆ Set the uprights edge-to-edge with the ends aligned on a worktable and clamp one piece down. Starting 2 inches from the bottom, outline four $\frac{3}{4}$-inch-wide, 3-inch-long dadoes 12 inches apart on each piece. Tack a board across the uprights as a router guide for each dado (page 11).

◆ Adjust a router's bit depth to $\frac{1}{4}$ inch, then cut the dadoes.

◆ Saw a notch $\frac{3}{8}$- by $\frac{1}{4}$-inch deep at the back corners of each tread so they will fit over the rounded ends of the dadoes, as shown at right.

◆ With a saber saw, round off the top corners of the uprights and sand them smooth.

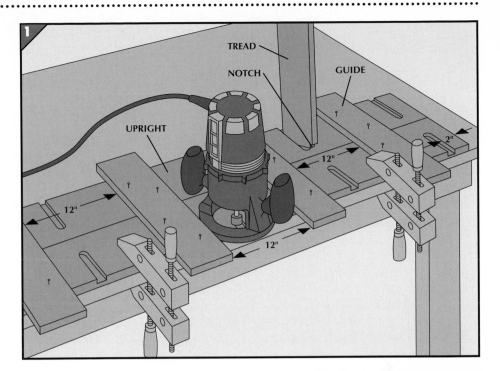

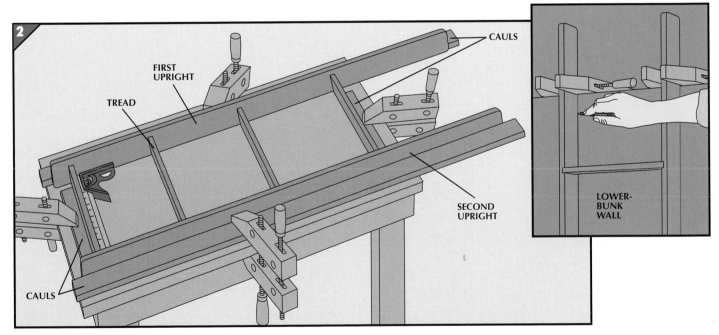

2. Assembling the ladder.

◆ To hold the ladder parts in place, clamp a straight board slightly longer than the uprights to a worktable as a caul.

◆ Spread glue in the dadoes in the uprights and on the ends of the treads, then stand one of the uprights on edge with the open ends of the dadoes down and butt the upright against the caul.

◆ Fit the treads into the dadoes, then position the second upright against the dadoes.

◆ With a combination square, check that the top and bottom treads are perpendicular to the uprights, then clamp short cauls to the table to hold the treads and uprights square.

◆ Clamp another long caul to the table firmly against the second upright (above). Let the glue dry.

◆ Attach a handscrew clamp to each upright to suspend the ladder from the bunk bed's lower wall and mark each edge of both uprights (inset).

◆ Remove the ladder and, between each pair of marked lines, drill five clearance holes for $1\frac{1}{2}$-inch No. 10 wood screws through the lower-bunk wall.

◆ Replace the ladder with the clamps still on it and, while a helper holds it steady, drill countersunk pilot holes into the uprights from the other side of the lower-bunk wall.

◆ Attach the ladder to the wall with washers and screws.

A Murphy-Bed Storage Cabinet

In a small bedroom, den, or guest room, a freestanding bed would squander valuable floor space. Most of this area can be used for other purposes if you substitute a fold-down bed, commonly called a Murphy bed after the man who patented the first one in 1925, that vanishes between two cabinets when it is not in use. Such units can be constructed to fit twin (39- by 75-inch), double (54- by 75-inch), or queen (60- by 80-inch) mattresses.

Attaching the Bed: At the center of the system is a pair of two-piece spring boxes supplied by the bed manufacturer. One part of each box attaches to the bed frame and the other to the cabinets. When the foot of the bed is lifted, the spring-box mechanism helps draw the bed upright.

 TOOLS

Router
Circular saw
Carpenter's
  level
Bar clamps
Electric drill
Hammer
Screwdriver

 **MATERIALS**

Plywood ($\frac{3}{4}$")
Shelf standards
Wood screws
  ($1\frac{1}{4}$" No. 8)
Finishing nails
  ($\frac{1}{2}$", 1")
Fold-down bed
  hardware

Drawer glides
Wood glue
Bifold doors
Magnetic latches
Surface-mounted
  hinges
Edge banding
Tack-on molding

 SAFETY TIPS

Protect your eyes with safety goggles when hammering.

A fold-down bed with cabinets.

The unit at right has a pair of cabinets designed for bedside storage, with drawers as well as both fixed and adjustable shelves. Sized 84 inches tall and 16 inches deep, the cabinets are connected by a continuous top and spaced 64 inches apart to house a queen-size bed and hardware. The mounting plates of the two spring boxes are fastened to the cabinets, and the hinge parts are attached to the sides of the bed. When stowed away, the mattress is hidden by a pair of bifold doors that fold flat against the cabinets when the bed is in the down position. Magnetic catches keep the doors closed when the bed is upright.

ADJUSTABLE
SHELF

TOP

MAGNETIC
CATCH

TACK-ON
MOLDING

FIXED
SHELF

SPRING-BOX
HINGE

SPRING-BOX
MOUNTING PLATE

BIFOLD DOORS

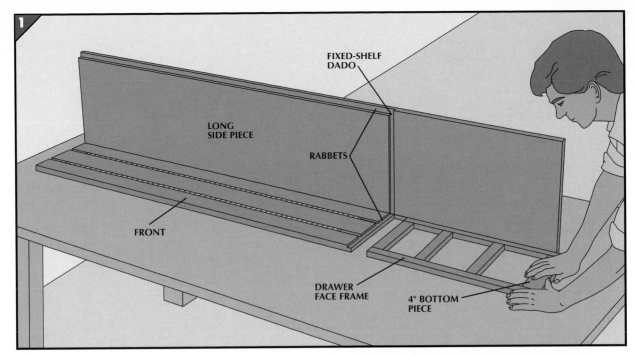

FIXED-SHELF DADO

LONG SIDE PIECE

RABBETS

FRONT

DRAWER FACE FRAME

4" BOTTOM PIECE

1. Cutting and fitting the cabinets.
◆ For each unit, cut a front and back piece 12 inches wide and 60 inches long, then rout a $\frac{3}{4}$-inch rabbet *(page 10)* along the bottoms of the pieces.
◆ Cut one side piece 16 inches wide and 84 inches long, and the opposite one 16 inches wide and 24 inches long. For the fixed shelf, rout a $\frac{3}{4}$-inch dado *(page 11)* across the longer piece 24 inches from the bottom. Cut $\frac{3}{4}$-inch rabbets along one long edge of the shorter piece and along both long edges of the taller piece, stopping the cut on the back edge at the fixed-shelf dado.
◆ Fasten shelf standards to the inner faces of the front and back panels *(page 59, Step 1)*.
◆ Keeping the tops of the pieces flush, fit the front into the full-length rabbet in the long side piece and fasten them together with $1\frac{1}{4}$-inch No. 8 wood screws driven every 12 inches.
◆ Build a face frame the same width as the front to hold the drawers: Cut the horizontal piece at the bottom 4 inches wide and all the other pieces 2 inches wide, then fasten them together in the same manner as the one on page 60, Step 3.
◆ Set the face frame against the end of the front and in the rabbet in the long side piece *(above)* and screw it in place.

BACK PANEL

SHORT SIDE PIECE

2. Attaching the back panel.
◆ Fit the rabbet in the short side piece against the face frame and screw it in place.
◆ Attach the back panel to the rabbet in the long side piece with screws driven every 12 inches *(left)*.
◆ Make a fixed shelf to fit into the front, side, and back pieces, and glue and screw it in place.

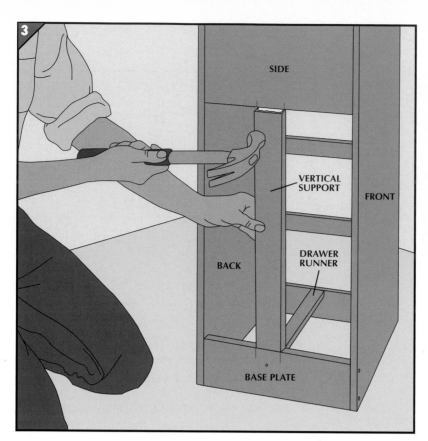

SIDE

VERTICAL
SUPPORT

FRONT

BACK

DRAWER
RUNNER

BASE PLATE

3. Completing the drawer units.

◆ Cut a 6-inch wide base plate to fit between the front and back pieces, and attach it with a pair of screws at each end.

◆ Fasten a 2-inch-wide strip as a drawer runner between the base plate and the lowest drawer face-frame piece with a pair of 1-inch finishing nails, checking with a carpenter's level that it is horizontal and flush with the top edge of the face frame.

◆ Cut a 2-inch-wide vertical support piece, spread wood glue on its ends, and gently tap it into place between the base plate and the bottom edge of the side panel *(left)*.

◆ Attach two more drawer runners to the vertical support at the horizontal face-frame pieces.

◆ Make the drawers *(page 13)* and cut adjustable shelves.

4. Mounting the spring boxes.

◆ Position the drawer units in their approximate positions in the room, then remove the locking clip from each spring box and separate the mounting plate from the hinge section.

◆ Place the mounting plate on its cabinet according to the manufacturer's instructions; for the model shown, the top edge of the plate is 16 inches from the floor. Checking that the plate is level, attach it to the cabinet with the screws provided *(right)*.

◆ Attach the hinge sections to the sides of the bed.

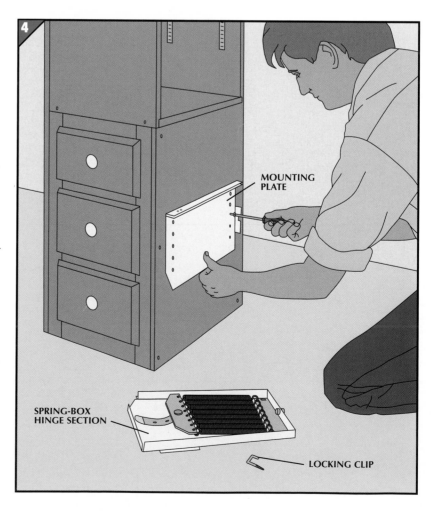

MOUNTING
PLATE

SPRING-BOX
HINGE SECTION

LOCKING CLIP

5. Attaching tack-on molding.

◆ Place the cabinets against the wall at the appropriate distance apart for the size of the bed, then locate and mark a stud behind each unit.

◆ Join the cabinets with a top *(page 65, Step 2)*, attaching the trim that wraps around it so the bottom edge is flush with its surface.

◆ Drill countersunk pilot holes through the back of the cabinets and into the studs every 12 to 16 inches, then drive in screws.

◆ Trim the outside bottom edges of the cabinets with 1-by-2 strips, beveling the tops at a 15-degree angle and mitering the outside corner joints.

◆ Find and mark the center of each cabinet front panel 6 inches from its top and bottom ends.

◆ Attach two center pieces of tack-on molding to the panel at the marks with $\frac{1}{2}$-inch finishing nails, then nail on a curved side piece at each end of the center piece.

◆ Cut two long side pieces to fit between the curved ones, then attach them to the cabinet *(right)*.

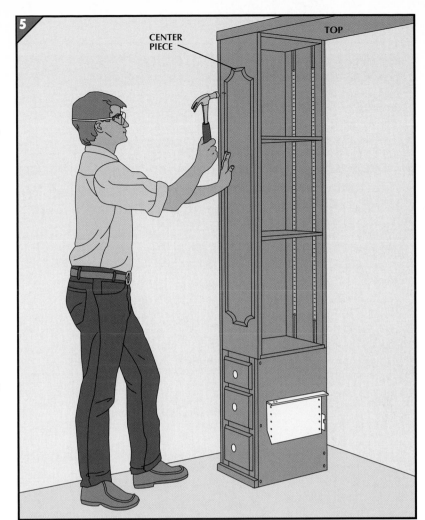

6. Hanging the doors.

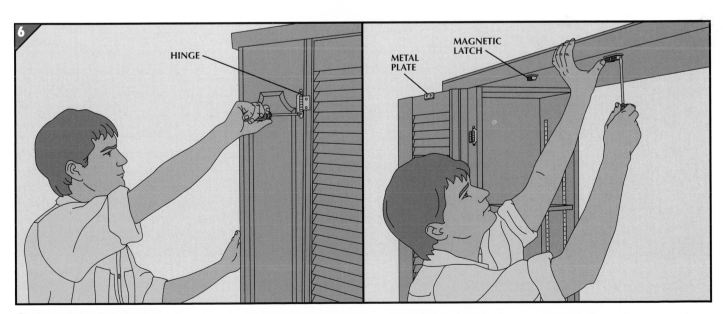

◆ Buy a set of bifold doors to fit the opening between the cabinets.

◆ Attach surface-mounted cabinet hinges to the edge of the doors about 10 inches from the top and bottom *(page 48, Step 3)*, then screw the hinges to the cabinet *(above, left)*.

◆ Screw the metal plate of a magnetic door-catch assembly to the inside of each door, centered along the top end. Close the doors and mark the plate positions on the top.

◆ Fasten a latch to the underside of the top at each mark with the screws provided *(above, right)*.

◆ Working with a helper, slide the hinge sections on the bed into their mounting plates on the cabinets, then install the locking clips.

3

Streamlining the Kitchen

Valuable storage space is often squandered in kitchens because of poor cabinet design or layout. Without remodeling the whole kitchen, you can turn these wasted areas to your advantage by reorganizing cabinet interiors or dedicating floor space to a custom-built island. To solve ironing-board storage problems, build a permanent ironing surface that disappears into a wall.

Hanging a corner-cabinet storage unit →

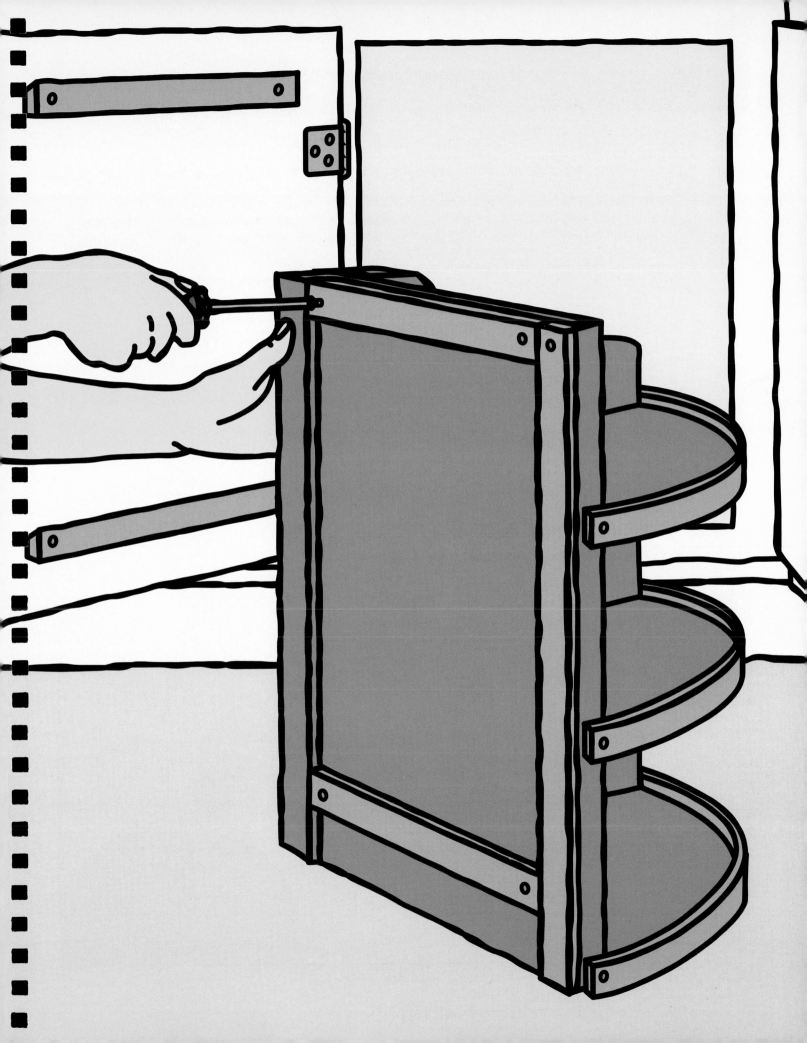

Reorganizing Cupboard Space

Kitchen cabinets with doors and deep shelves make poor containers for small, flat objects, just as units with drawers are unsuitable for storing china. But if your kitchen cabinets do not match your present needs, you need not build new units. With simple carpentry and inexpensive hardware, you can substitute shelves for drawers in one cabinet—installing a partition and a bottom, if necessary—or switch from shelves to drawers in another.

Emptying the Interior: Before you can fashion most interior improvements, you will have to gut the cabinet. The job may be simple: To clear away doors, drawers on metal glides, or shelves on metal brackets, you need only unscrew the supporting hardware. Wood mountings are harder to dismantle; some can be unscrewed, but many are glued in place. These mountings can be sawed into pieces, then knocked away from the cabinet sides or partitions with a hammer. Remaining nailheads can be cut off and cavities filled with wood putty. A keyhole saw is handy for cutting inside the confined reaches of a cabinet.

 TOOLS

Keyhole saw	Carpenter's level
Hammer	Saber saw
Tape measure	Carpenter's nippers
Combination square	Electric drill

 **MATERIALS**

Sandpaper (60, 100, 150 grit)	Wood screws ($1\frac{1}{4}$" No. 8)
Wood putty	Drawer glides
1 x 1s, 1 x 2s	Plywood ($\frac{1}{2}$", $\frac{3}{4}$")
Wood glue	

 SAFETY TIPS

Wear goggles when you are sawing inside a cabinet, using a power tool, or hammering.

SWITCHING FROM DRAWERS TO SHELVES

1. Gutting the interior.

◆ Remove the drawers and, with a keyhole saw, cut the horizontal rails from the face frame just inside the drawer guides and supports, leaving short stubs you can cut off later.
◆ If a support piece is glued to the front and back of the cabinet as well as to the side, cut it in half *(right)*. Take out all nails and screws holding the supports and guides in place.
◆ Break the glue bonds by tapping the guides and supports with a hammer, and pull out the pieces.
◆ Cut the rail stubs as close to the edges of the face frame as you can without scratching it. With 60-grit sandpaper, sand the cut ends flush. Repeat with 100- and 150-grit paper.
◆ Fill any cavities left after sanding with wood putty, let the putty dry, and sand the surface smooth.

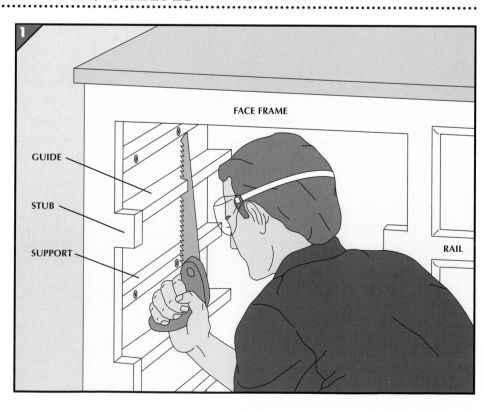

2. Fastening partition cleats.

◆ Cut two 1-by-1 cleats to the interior height of the cabinet for each stile of the face frame.
◆ To position the back cleat, transfer the locations of the top and bottom corners of the stile at the front of the opening to the back of the cabinet with a combination square and a straight board *(inset)*, then draw a vertical line $\frac{1}{2}$ inch outside of the marks *(dashed line)*.

◆ Spread wood glue on one edge of the back cleat, position it against the back of the cabinet along the vertical line, and fasten it in place with three $1\frac{1}{4}$-inch No. 8 wood screws *(above)*.
◆ Mount the other cleat to the inside face of the stile $\frac{1}{2}$ inch away from the opening

3. Installing the partition and shelves.

◆ Make a partition from $\frac{1}{2}$-inch plywood to the height and depth of the cabinet's interior.
◆ Spread glue on the inner edges of the cleats, then screw the partition in place *(above, left)*.
◆ Glue and screw a horizontal 1-by-1 cleat to the cabinet front with its top edge $\frac{1}{2}$ inch below the door opening.
◆ Use a level to draw lines on the side wall and partition

at the same height as the front cleat, and secure side cleats along these lines *(above, right)*.
◆ Cut a bottom from $\frac{1}{2}$-inch plywood, then glue and screw it to the cleats in the same manner as you did the partition.
◆ Install side cleats to support each shelf, then cut and install shelves on them.
◆ Fit the cabinet with a door *(pages 48-49 or page 61)*.

CHANGING SHELVES TO DRAWERS

1. Clearing the space.

◆ To remove shelves glued into dadoes, fit a saber saw with a flush-cutting blade and cut a V from the front edge to the back of the shelf *(right)*. If the shelf extends through more than one section of the cabinet, make V cuts in each section, then saw lengthwise along the middle of the shelf to connect the Vs.

◆ Tap the top and bottom of the remaining shelf pieces with a hammer to break the glue bond, then gently work them free.

◆ Where you have cut shelves that run through more than one section, install a partition between the sections *(page 95, Steps 2 and 3)*.

To remove a shelf mounted on cleats, take out any nails or screws from the shelf and tap it from below to break the glue bond. Unscrew the cleats and tap them to break the glue bond. Snip off protruding nail or screws with carpenter's nippers.

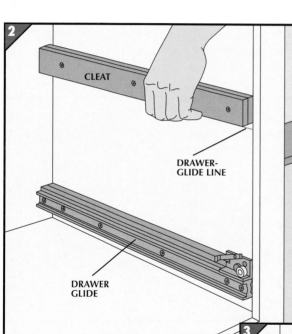

2. Mounting drawer glides.

◆ Determine the height of the drawers and mark their glide positions on both cabinet side walls *(page 62, Step 1)*.

◆ For each glide on the bottom drawer, cut two 1-by-2 cleats and fasten them to the cabinet along their drawer-glide marks *(page 63, Step 3)*.

◆ Separate the drawer glides into their pieces and screw the ones that attach to the cabinet against the cleats.

◆ Mount cleats and glides for the remaining drawers in the same way *(left)*.

3. Installing the drawers.

◆ Build the drawers in a similar manner as the ones on page 13, Step 1, but in this instance omit the false fronts.

◆ Fasten glides to each side of the drawers; for the model shown, position each glide so the roller is flush with the drawer's bottom edge.

◆ To insert the drawers, slip the rollers into the glides mounted to the cabinet *(right)* and push the drawer into the cabinet.

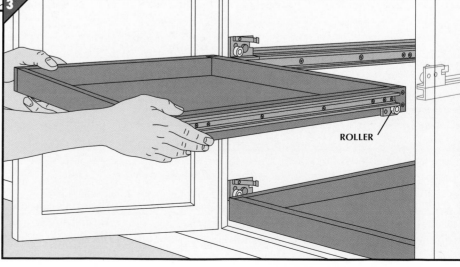

Door-and-Trolley Corner Storage

Corners in kitchen cabinets can be difficult, if not impossible, to access. You can take full advantage of these hard-to-reach areas by building a door-hung storage unit and a rolling trolley that tucks into the corner when it is not needed *(below)*. Before you begin, remove existing shelves from the corner section to make room *(page 96, Step 1)*. If you will be storing heavy items on the shelves, add a third door hinge between the other two.

The Trolley Unit: Build the trolley like the rolling cabinet on page 29, but with two fixed shelves instead of a false top and drawer, and use nonswiveling casters. Make the depth of the trolley slightly narrower than the opening, and its height—minus the wheels—about 3 inches shorter so you can lift the wheels over the bottom of the cabinet to get it in place.

 TOOLS

Circular saw
Router
Saber saw
Compass
Screwdriver
C-clamps
Bar clamp
Wood chisel
Mallet
Table saw

 **MATERIALS**

Plywood ($\frac{3}{4}$")
Bendable plywood ($\frac{1}{4}$")
Wood trim ($\frac{1}{4}$" x 1")
Edge banding
Wood screws
  ($\frac{3}{4}$" No. 5,
  1" No. 4,
  1$\frac{1}{4}$" No. 8)
Nonswiveling casters
Wood glue

SAFETY TIPS

Prevent eye injury by wearing goggles when you are using a power tool.

An accessible corner unit.

This unique solution to corner-cabinet storage consists of a quarter-round door unit and a rolling trolley inside the cabinet. When the door is swung open, the trolley can be wheeled to the front for access *(inset)*. The back of the door unit fits in a dado *(page 11)* cut in the side piece $\frac{1}{4}$ inch from its inner edge, and the side has a curved cutout to ease access to the trolley. The curved shelves sit in matching dadoes and a rabbet *(page 10)* in the back and side, and each shelf has an edging strip at the front to keep items from falling out. The unit is secured to the door by interlocking beveled ledgers *(page 99)*. To ensure that the door will close properly, make the back and sides of the quarter-round unit 1$\frac{1}{2}$ inches smaller all around than the opening, and the radius of the curved shelves slightly less than the width of the back and sides.

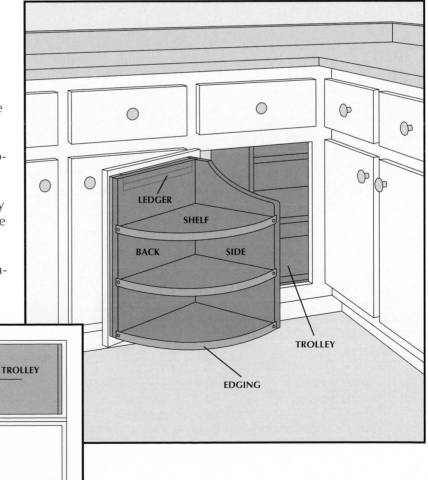

MAKING AND MOUNTING THE DOOR UNIT

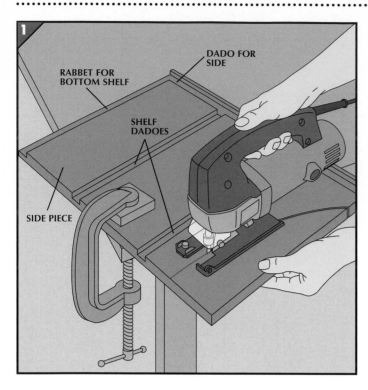

1. Preparing the back and side.
◆ From $\frac{3}{4}$-inch furniture-grade plywood, cut the side and back pieces $1\frac{1}{2}$ inches smaller all around than the opening, then rout a $\frac{3}{4}$-inch-wide dado *(page 11)* along the length of the side, $\frac{1}{4}$ inch from one edge, to hold the back piece.
◆ On each piece, cut a $\frac{3}{4}$-inch-wide rabbet *(page 10)* along the bottom for the bottom shelf and $\frac{3}{4}$-inch-wide dadoes one-third and two-thirds of the way up for the middle and top shelves. Measure carefully to make sure the dadoes on both pieces align and stop the cuts in the side at the back dado.
◆ Mark a curve on the top outer corner of the side, then clamp the piece to a worktable, and make the cut with a saber saw *(left)*.
◆ Cut a $\frac{1}{4}$-inch notch *(page 11, Step 3)* at the end of each shelf dado and rabbet to accommodate edging.

2. Attaching the shelves.
◆ Fit the back piece into the dado in the side piece and fasten them together with three $1\frac{1}{4}$-inch screws.
◆ Cut three square shelves slightly larger than the width of the side, then adjust a compass to a radius $\frac{1}{4}$ inch less than the side's width.
◆ With the compass point at one corner of a shelf, scribe a curve on the surface, then cut along the curve with a saber saw.
◆ Cut the other two shelves using the first as a template, then

screw them to the dadoes in the sides and back.
◆ For each shelf, cut a strip of $\frac{1}{4}$-inch bendable plywood to fit as edging between the notches in the back and sides. Apply wood glue to one face of the strip, secure one end to the shelf with a bar clamp so its bottom edge is flush with the shelf's underside, then attach the other end to the shelf with a 1-inch No. 4 screw *(right)*. Remove the clamp and fasten the other end of the strip.

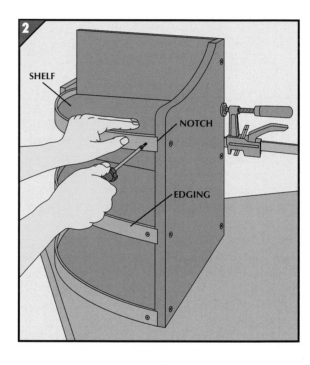

TRICKS OF THE TRADE

Cutting Multiple Curves

Save time by cutting three curved shelves in one operation rather than individually. Stack the pieces together with double-sided tape so the edges of the pieces are aligned. Scribe the curve on the top piece, then clamp the stack to a worktable with the cutting line extending off the surface. Cut the curve with a saber saw.

3. Hanging the unit.

◆ Cut four strips of $\frac{1}{4}$- by 1-inch wood trim $1\frac{3}{4}$ inches shorter than the width of the back piece as ledgers, then make a 45-degree bevel in one edge of each strip. Cut another strip as long as the height of the back as a filler strip.

◆ Position one ledger against the back of the cabinet door 2 inches from the top, centered between the edges, beveled-edge up; attach it with a pair of $\frac{3}{4}$-inch No. 5 screws. Fasten a second ledger 3 inches from the bottom of the door.

◆ Attach the filler strip to the back of the unit along the outer edge of the back.

◆ Fasten the third ledger bevel-side down to the back of the unit $2\frac{1}{2}$ inches from the bottom. Attach the last ledger to the back piece flush with the top *(right)*.

◆ Hang the unit on the door so the bevels of the ledgers interlock *(inset)*.

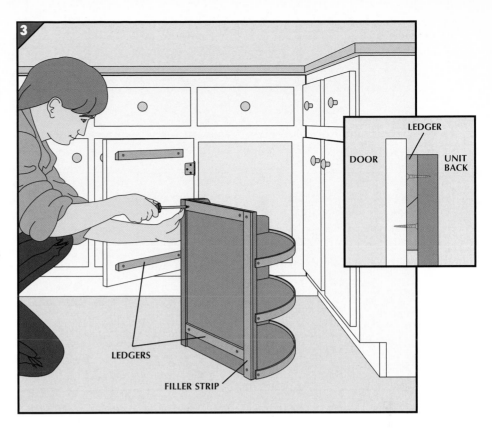

LEDGERS

FILLER STRIP

LEDGER

DOOR   LEDGER   UNIT BACK

BUILDING THE TROLLEY

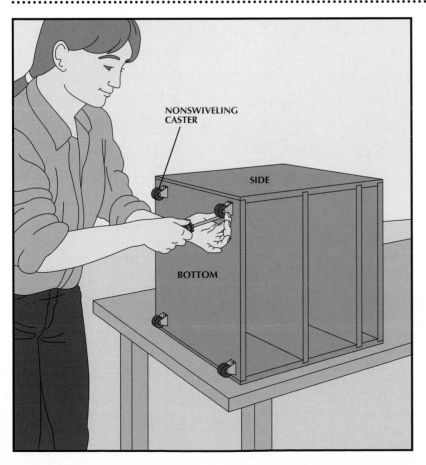

NONSWIVELING CASTER

SIDE

BOTTOM

Attaching the wheels.

◆ Build the trolley as you would the rolling cabinet on page 29, joining the top and bottom to the sides with rabbets and screws, but omit the false top and drawer and mount two fixed shelves in dadoes.

◆ Set the trolley on one side and position a nonswiveling caster on the bottom 2 inches from one corner.

◆ Mark the screw holes and attach the caster with the screws provided.

◆ Fasten a caster to each remaining corner in the same way *(left)*.

A Slide-and-Turn Spice Rack

When spice jars are stored in a kitchen cabinet, they occupy horizontal space on a shelf but leave most of the vertical area above them unusable. A pull-out rack will keep spice jars neatly arranged and easily accessible, and at the same time allow tall items to be stored on the other cabinet shelves.

Hardware: The rack is fastened to the divider with a type of hardware commonly used on pocket doors in cabinets. The hardware kit has a pair of slide rails and two hinges, and is available for right- or left-hand installations. It can be obtained from specialty hardware stores or ordered from catalogs.

 TOOLS

Circular saw	Screwdriver
Router	Hammer
Saber saw	Hacksaw
Electric drill	Carpenter's
C-clamps	square
Bar clamps	

 **MATERIALS**

Furniture-grade plywood ($\frac{3}{4}$")
Wood trim ($\frac{1}{4}$" x 1")
Wood glue
Wood screws ($1\frac{1}{4}$" No. 8)
Finishing nails (1")
Pocket-door hardware kit

 SAFETY TIPS

Wear goggles to protect your eyes when you are using a power tool.

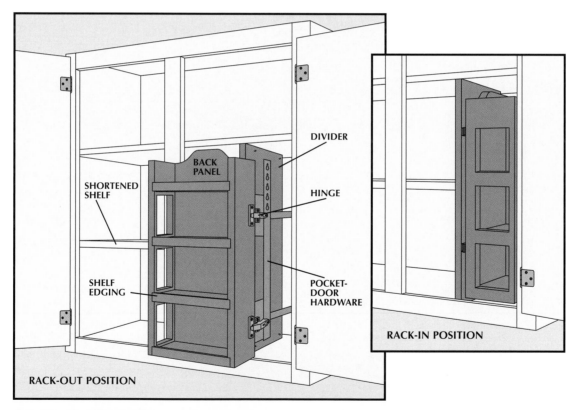

SHORTENED SHELF

BACK PANEL

DIVIDER

HINGE

SHELF EDGING

POCKET-DOOR HARDWARE

RACK-OUT POSITION

RACK-IN POSITION

A pull-out spice rack.

The rack shown above is mounted on a divider with pocket-door hardware and, when fully opened, turns to 90 degrees on a pair of European hinges included with the hardware kit. It consists of four 4-inch-deep shelves spaced about 5 inches apart to accommodate two rows of average-size spice jars on each shelf. (If you prefer, you can space one or more shelves at different heights for taller or shorter items.) The back panel, with a decorative cut along the top, is 3 inches narrower than the depth of the cabinet to provide enough clearance for the rack to fit in its stored position *(inset)*. The back panel is glued into rabbets *(page 10)* in the side pieces and the bottom shelf fits in rabbets at the bottoms of the sides and back. Dadoes *(page 11)* cut into the sides and back hold the remaining shelves. To keep jars from falling out, wood edging is glued along the front of the shelves.

PUTTING THE RACK TOGETHER

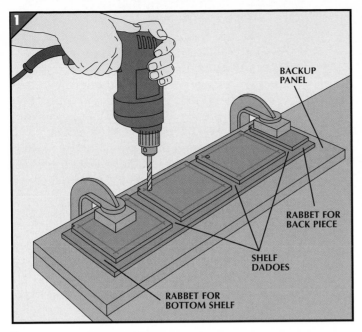

BACKUP PANEL

RABBET FOR BACK PIECE

SHELF DADOES

RABBET FOR BOTTOM SHELF

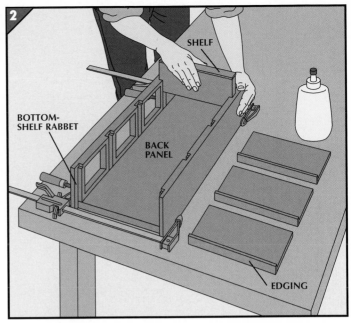

SHELF

BOTTOM-SHELF RABBET

BACK PANEL

EDGING

1. Preparing the pieces.

◆ Trim the sides from $\frac{3}{4}$-inch furniture-grade plywood, then cut a $\frac{3}{4}$-inch-wide rabbet *(page 10)* along the bottom and one edge of each piece. Cut a dado *(page 11)* across each side every 5 inches.
◆ Cut $\frac{1}{4}$-inch notches at the tops of the rabbets and dadoes *(page 11, Step 3)* to accommodate the shelf trim.
◆ Outline a rectangular opening on one side between the shelf positions, clamp the piece to a worktable atop a back-up panel, and drill a $\frac{1}{2}$-inch hole through the side at a point along the inner edge of each outline *(above)*.
◆ Insert the blade of a saber saw in the hole and cut out the opening.

2. Assembling the rack.

◆ Cut the back panel to size, then outline and cut a decorative arc across the top so its edges will be flush with those of the sides.
◆ Spread wood glue in the edge rabbets in the side pieces, fit the back and sides together so the bottom of the back is flush with the top of the bottom-shelf rabbet in the sides, and secure the assembly with a pair of bar clamps.
◆ Trim four shelves 1 inch narrower than the sides to fit between the sides. Cut four pieces of shelf edging from $\frac{1}{4}$- by 1-inch wood trim to the same length as the shelves.
◆ Tack the trim to the shelves with 1-inch finishing nails so the bottom edges of the strips are flush with the shelves' undersides, spread glue in the dadoes and rabbet in the sides, and slide the shelves into place *(above)*.

MOUNTING THE ASSEMBLY

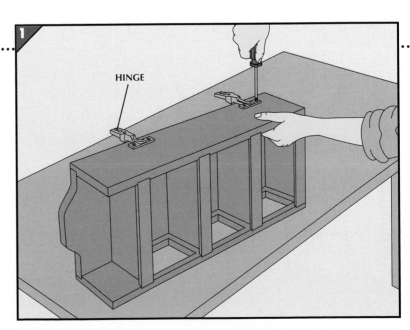

HINGE

1. Attaching the hinges.

◆ Position the hinges supplied with a pocket-door hardware kit on the solid side of the rack, following the manufacturer's instructions. For the model shown, two European hinges *(page 48)* are placed along the back edge of the side, one near the top and one near the bottom.
◆ Mark the screw holes and attach the hinges to the rack with the screws supplied *(right)*.

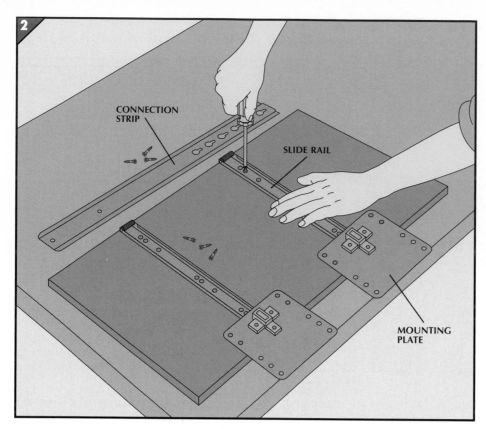

CONNECTION STRIP

SLIDE RAIL

MOUNTING PLATE

2. Outfitting the divider.

◆ Cut the vertical divider to fit between the bottom and second shelf of the cabinet, making it as wide as the cabinet depth.

◆ Place the rack against the divider so their bottoms are flush and mark the hinges on the side of the divider to which the rack will be attached.

◆ Position the door-hardware slide rails across the divider along the hinge marks so their ends align with the edges of the divider; cut the rails to length with a hacksaw, if necessary.

◆ Checking that the rails are perpendicular to the divider's ends with a carpenter's square, mark the screw holes, then drive the screws supplied *(left)*.

◆ Screw the connection strip to the mounting plates, driving a screw in each round hole and one in the appropriate oblong hole.

3. Installing the divider.

◆ Remove the first shelf from the cabinet.

◆ Hinge the rack to the divider mounting plates, and fit the assembly into the cabinet. Mark the divider's position on the bottom and top shelves.

◆ Cut the first shelf to fit against the divider, and mark its position on the divider.

◆ Take the rack out, unhinge it from the divider, then add dadoes, shelf standards *(page 59, Step 1)*, or shelf-pin holes *(page 21, Step 1)* on the side of the divider that will support the end of the shortened shelf.

◆ Position the divider in the cabinet, holding it in place with a small bar clamp secured to the top shelf.

◆ Fix the bottom of the divider with a pair of $1\frac{1}{4}$-inch No. 8 wood screws driven at an angle through the panel into the bottom of the cabinet, then attach the top of the divider to the top shelf in the same way *(right)*.

◆ Secure the rack to the divider by screwing it to the hinges, then set the shortened shelf in place.

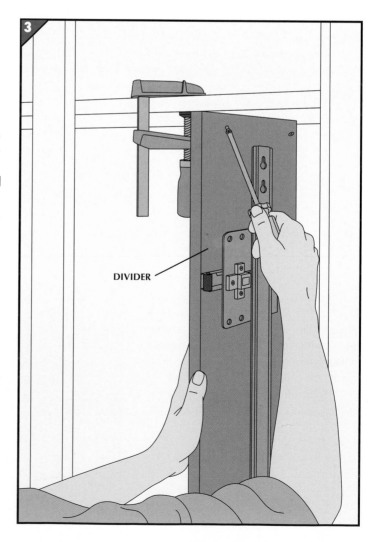

DIVIDER

An Ironing Board in a Wall Cupboard

Awkward to store and a nuisance to set up every day, an ironing board can be kept out of sight but close at hand in a convenient cupboard that is recessed between two wall studs. When it is not needed, the board folds up easily to be hidden away behind a door. Related supplies and accessories such as the iron and a spray bottle can be housed on shelves within the cabinet.

Sizing the Parts: For a typical wall with 2-by-4 studs at 16-inch intervals, the cabinet frame will be $14\frac{1}{2}$ inches wide, and should extend about 2 inches beyond the wall surface in order to accommodate supplies on the shelves. With this depth, the cabinet sides will be about 6 inches deep. Mount the board at a comfortable height—a standard ironing board is about 34 inches tall, but you can

place one at a different height if desired. The board on these pages occupies less space than the standard 54-inch model, but if you choose a nonstandard length, you will need to make a cover to fit it or alter an existing one.

 When cutting into walls, take precautions against releasing lead and asbestos particles into the air (page 45).

CAUTION

 TOOLS

Compass
Carpenter's square
Saber saw
Bar clamps
Screwdriver
Electric drill
Circular saw

MATERIALS

Furniture-grade plywood ($\frac{3}{4}$")
Hardwood (1" x 1")
Strap hinge (3")
Wooden dowel (1")
Wood screws ($\frac{3}{4}$", $1\frac{1}{4}$" No. 8)
Sandpaper (medium grade)
European door hinges (170°)

 SAFETY TIPS

Wear safety goggles when working with power tools.

Anatomy of an ironing cupboard.

The cabinet at right is made of $\frac{3}{4}$-inch furniture-grade plywood and is sized to fit between adjacent wall studs and between the wall's baseboard and top plate. The top and bottom pieces rest in $\frac{3}{4}$-inch-wide rabbets *(page 10)* cut in the ends of the side pieces, and the three fixed shelves are held in dadoes *(page 11)* in the sides. The door has 170-degree self-closing European hinges that allow it to fold back flat against the wall. A 48-inch board sits 30 to 35 inches above the floor and, when folded up *(inset)*, rotates on a 1-inch dowel set in holes drilled in the sides. In the down position, the board is supported by a 1-by-1 leg with a two-piece foot. The leg is attached to the board with a strap hinge fastened to a cleat on the underside of the board.

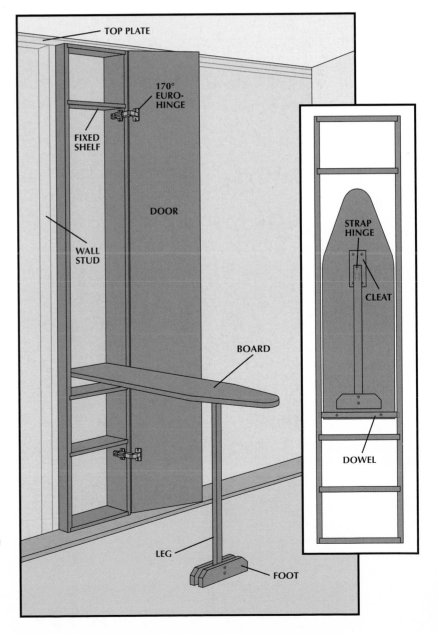

1. Making the board.

◆ Cut a piece of $\frac{3}{4}$-inch furniture-grade plywood 12 inches wide to length.
◆ Make a mark at the center of the board 4 inches from the top. With a compass set to a radius of 4 inches and the point at the center mark, scribe a circle on the board *(right)*.
◆ Mark each edge of the board 16 inches from the top, then extend the marks to the circle with a carpenter's square *(dashed lines)*.
◆ Cut along the lines with a saber saw, then smooth the cut edges with medium-grade sandpaper.

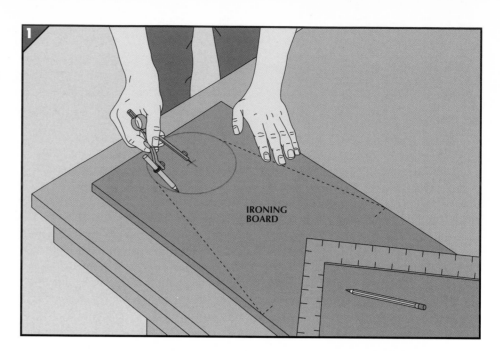

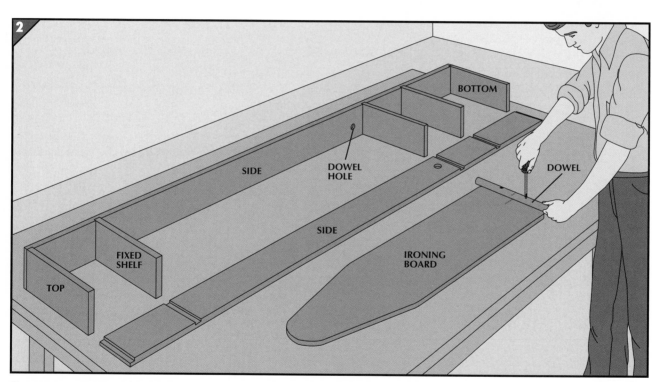

2. Assembling the closet.

◆ Cut the top, bottom, and side pieces to size, then rout $\frac{3}{4}$-inch-wide rabbets *(page 10)* along the ends of the sides.
◆ Make $\frac{3}{4}$-inch-wide dadoes *(page 11)* across the side pieces at each shelf location, measuring carefully to ensure that the cuts align.
◆ Mark the middle of each side piece at the desired ironing-board height and drill a $\frac{3}{8}$-inch-deep

hole at each mark *(page 16, Step 1)* with a 1-inch spade bit.
◆ Fit the top, bottom, and fixed shelves into one of the side pieces, then cut a 1-inch dowel $13\frac{1}{2}$ inches long.
◆ Mark the centers of the dowel and the ironing board's straight end, place the dowel at the bottom of the board with the marks aligned, and a drill pilot hole for a $1\frac{1}{4}$-inch No. 8 wood screw on

each side of the center through the dowel and into the board.
◆ Drive the screws to fasten the dowel to the board *(above)*.
◆ Fit the dowel into its hole in one side, then set the opposite side into place.
◆ Secure the assembly with a pair of bar clamps and attach the top, bottom, and fixed shelves to the sides with two screws at each joint.

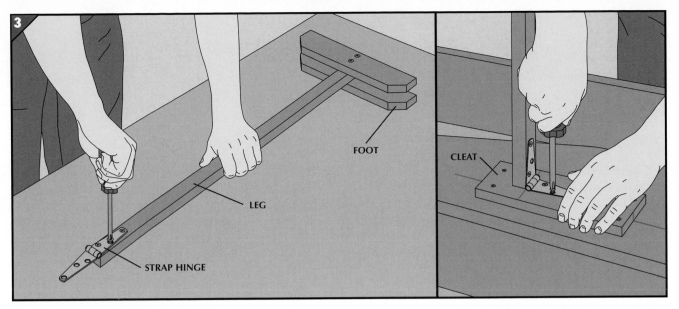

3. Attaching the leg to the board.

◆ Cut a length of 1-by-1 hardwood $1\frac{1}{2}$ inches shorter than the ironing-board height.

◆ Trim two plywood strips 3 inches wide and 11 inches long, then cut 30-degree miters across the top corners of each strip.

◆ Screw the feet to opposite sides of the leg so the bottoms are flush.

◆ Fasten a 3-inch strap hinge at the other end of the leg with three $\frac{3}{4}$-inch screws so the hinge pin aligns with the end of the leg (above, left).

◆ Cut a plywood cleat 10 inches long and 3 inches wide, then, with two $1\frac{1}{4}$-inch screws at each end, attach it to the middle of the underside of the board 12 inches from the curved end.

◆ Make a mark on the cleat 3 inches from the top, stand the leg on the cleat so the hinge pin aligns with the mark, and screw the hinge to the cleat (above, right).

4. Installing the closet.

◆ Cut an opening in the wall between two studs, the top plate, and the baseboard (page 72, Step 1).

◆ With a helper, stand the closet up and fit it into the opening.

◆ Anchor the closet to the wall studs and top plate with a $1\frac{1}{4}$-inch screw every 12 inches (left).

◆ Cut a door to the outside dimensions of the closet, and hang the door by attaching the bodies of a pair of 170-degree self-closing European hinges to it (page 48) 12 inches from the top and bottom. Fasten the mounting plates (page 49, Step 4) to the inner face of one side of the closet.

A Wine-Storage Island

When kitchen cabinets are not large enough for your needs, consider building a handy "island" to extend their area. The one shown on these pages is designed to include a wine rack and cutting board that would normally take up valuable space on a kitchen countertop.

The cabinet below is sized to hold 24 standard-size bottles of wine in tubes made from 4-inch polyvinyl-chloride (PVC) drainpipe, but you can alter the dimensions to suit your needs. To do so, first create the number of tubes you

want by cutting the PVC into 9-inch lengths. Set the tubes on end and group them in the arrangement they will be in the cabinet, then measure the group's dimensions to determine the width and height of the wine-storage compartment. Size the other sections of the cabinet in relation to these dimensions. Although the PVC tubes will be mostly concealed, you may want to sand off the printing on their sides or paint them with an automotive lacquer before you install them.

 TOOLS

Hacksaw
Circular saw
Saber saw

Router
Bar clamps
Electric drill
Caulking gun
Screwdriver

 MATERIALS

PVC drainpipe (4")
Furniture-grade
  plywood ($\frac{3}{4}$")
Dowel (1")

2 x 3s
Wood trim
  ($\frac{3}{4}$" x $\frac{3}{4}$")
Wood screws
  (1$\frac{1}{4}$", 1$\frac{1}{2}$" No. 8)
Finishing nails (1$\frac{1}{4}$")

Drawer and
  door pulls
Door hinges
Cutting board
Shelf standards
Silicone caulk

 SAFETY TIPS

Protect your eyes with goggles when you are using a power tool or hammering.

FRONT VIEW

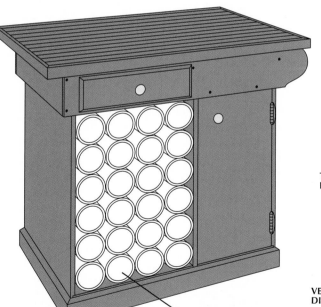

PVC DRAINPIPE

BACK VIEW

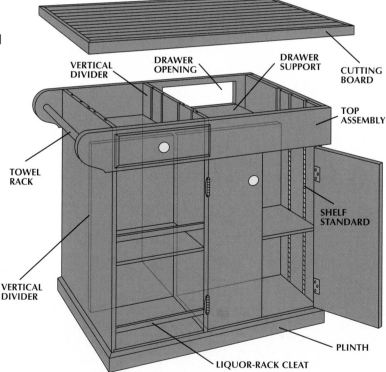

VERTICAL DIVIDER
DRAWER OPENING
DRAWER SUPPORT
CUTTING BOARD
TOP ASSEMBLY
TOWEL RACK
VERTICAL DIVIDER
SHELF STANDARD
LIQUOR-RACK CLEAT
PLINTH

Anatomy of a wine island.

The island above is a box with two sides and a bottom panel topped by an assembly that includes a cutting board, two drawers, and a towel rack. Two vertical dividers separate the box into four sections: a wine holder, an open liquor rack, and two compartments with adjustable shelves. The sections

are held in place with rabbets *(page 10)* and dadoes *(page 11)*, and the top assembly is fastened to the cabinet's sides and vertical divider. Doors are mounted with their faces flush with the front edges of the cabinet, and the entire unit sits in a rabbeted plinth made of 2-by-3s.

4. Hanging the door.

◆ Position one door on the closet opening and mark its corners on the face frame. Do the same with the other door, check the alignment, then adjust the door locations, if necessary.

◆ Reposition each door and screw the hinges to the face frame *(right)*.

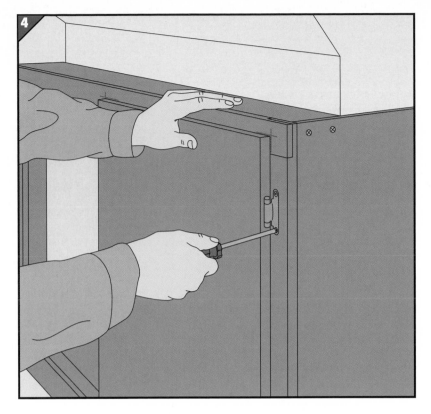

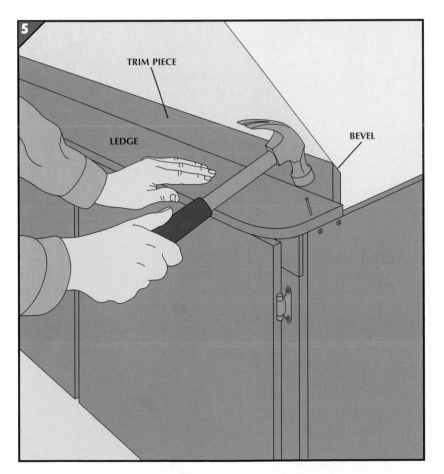

TRIM PIECE

LEDGE

BEVEL

5. Adding the trim.

◆ Cut a 6-inch-wide strip of $\frac{3}{4}$-inch plywood the length of the closet to serve as a ledge. With a saber saw, curve the front corner of the piece, then cover its exposed edges with edge banding *(page 12)*.

◆ Cut a $3\frac{1}{4}$-inch-wide plywood strip for a trim piece $\frac{3}{4}$ inch shorter than the ledge. On a table saw, bevel *(page 61, Step 1)* the top edge of the trim at the same angle as the ceiling *(page 47, Step 2)*.

◆ Attach the trim to the back edge of the ledge with $1\frac{1}{4}$-inch screws every 8 inches so the end opposite the dormer is aligned and the bottom edge of the trim is flush with the underside of the ledge.

◆ Position the ledge-trim assembly on the cabinet with the trim piece flush against the ceiling and attach the ledge to the cabinet face with three $1\frac{1}{2}$-inch finishing nails *(left)*.

◆ Cut a length of trim to fit along the dormer wall above the paneling and nail it to the studs.

◆ Cut and nail baseboard along the bottom of the closet and the paneling.

◆ Sink the nailheads with a nail set.

Under-Stairs Storage

Often overlooked, the space under a staircase can be organized into useful storage compartments. The triangular portion beneath the run of stairs is ideal for holding a stack of drawers, and the vertical area under a landing can be made into a closet.

Framing the Space: Align the closet's side wall directly under the junction between the landing and the stair stringers. Frame the closet using the techniques on pages 34 to 40, but for easier access to the shelves inside the closet, build the side wall with a stud at each end and no intermediate studs. Position the front-wall studs so that they can be covered with wallboard flush with the stair stringer.

Close off the closet with a flat-jamb door *(pages 54-55)* or with bifold doors *(pages 41-43)*. You can build the drawers to span the full height of the space, but for easy access, mount the top drawer at about eye level and the lowest one at knee height.

TOOLS

Line level
Screwdriver
Electric drill
Screwdriver bit
Carpenter's square

Carpenter's level
Nail set
Circular saw
Handsaw
T-bevel
Plumb bob
Pry bar

MATERIALS

1 x 1s, 1 x 2s
2 x 4s
Plywood ($\frac{3}{4}$")
Edging trim
($\frac{1}{2}$" x $\frac{1}{2}$")
Common nails (3")
Wood screws
(1$\frac{1}{4}$", 2$\frac{1}{2}$" No. 8)

Finishing nails
(1", 1$\frac{1}{2}$", 2")
Flat-jamb prehung
door
Doorknob kit
Wood shims
Wood putty
Light fixture and
wiring

SAFETY TIPS

Goggles protect your eyes when you are operating a power tool or hammering.

Storage under stairs.

This system has a closet under the stair landing and a column of drawers below the steps. A stud wall divides the two elements, and the drawers slide on plywood shelves held up by cleats fastened to the side-wall studs and to the stair stringers. (For a stairway with no landing, omit the closet and attach the drawer supports to the existing wall studs.) Runners guide the drawers, which have false fronts held in place by face frames at the front of the shelves. In this example, the space below the drawer column is framed by a subwall and the top drawers are omitted; these areas are left open to the closet. Wallboard covers the spaces around the drawers and wood trim conceals the wallboard edges.

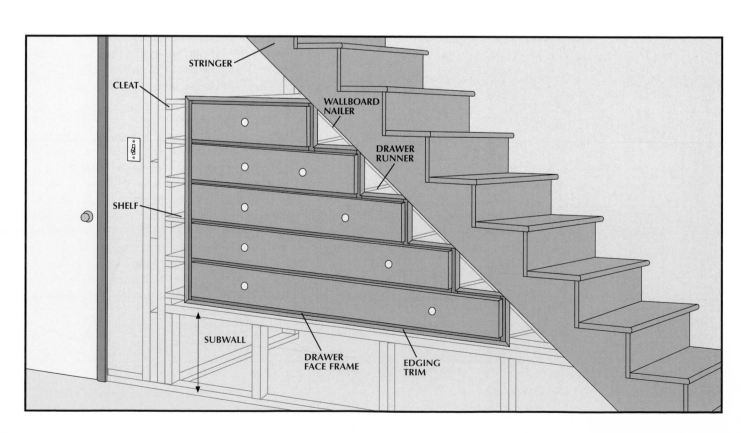

MOUNTING THE SHELVES AND DRAWERS

1. Starting the frame.
◆ Frame the walls for the closet *(pages 34-40)* under the staircase landing, placing the side wall at the junction between the landing and the stair stringers, and building this wall with only end studs, no intermediate studs. Align the front wall $\frac{1}{2}$ inch behind the face of the outer stringer to allow for the wallboard thickness.
◆ To mark the positions of the drawer shelves, first drive a nail at about eye level into the underside of a stair tread near the inner stringer. Run a string with a line level from the nail to the end stud of the closet side wall and make a level mark on the stud *(right)*.
◆ Repeat the process for the next five treads in descending order.
◆ Transfer the marks from the back stud to the front one with the line level.

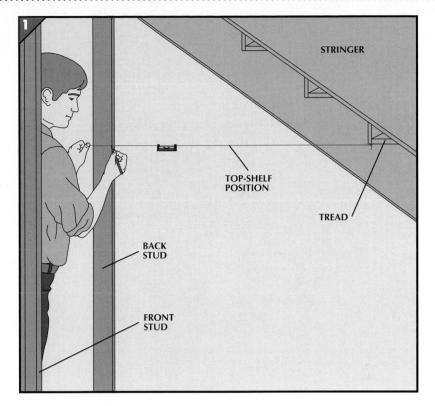

2. Installing shelf cleats.
◆ Cut six 1-by-1s to fit as cleats between the back wall and the front of the closet side wall. If the distance between the end studs exceeds 30 inches, use 1-by-2s.
◆ Hold the top cleat on the side-wall end studs at the shelf-position marks, drill a countersunk hole for a $1\frac{1}{4}$-inch No. 8 wood screw through it and into each stud, and fasten it in place.
◆ Mount the remaining cleats in the same way *(left)*.

3. Erecting the subwall.

◆ Measure the distance between the outer stringer and the front end stud of the closet side wall along the floor and at a point 22 inches above the floor.

◆ Copy the angle formed by the stringer and the floor with a T-bevel, then cut two 2-by-4s to the measured lengths as a top plate and a soleplate, beveling one end of each board at the angle of the stringer.

◆ Cut a 19-inch-long stud for each end of the subwall and every 16 inches in between, then fasten the studs to the plates with 3-inch common nails.

◆ Position the subwall on the floor flush with the front-wall framing of the closet. At one end, fasten the wall's end stud to the closet side wall with three $2\frac{1}{2}$-inch No. 8 wood screws *(left)*. At the other end, screw the soleplate to the floor and the top plate to the underside of the stringer.

4. Mounting the shelves.

◆ Stretch a level line from the top wall cleat to a stair riser, measure it, then cut a shelf from $\frac{3}{4}$-inch plywood to that length and wide enough to fit between the stair stringers. Do the same for five more shelves below the first.

◆ For each shelf except the top one, trim two 1-by-1s to the width of the shelf to serve as drawer runners. With three $1\frac{1}{4}$-inch screws, fasten one across the top of the shelf 6 inches from the side-wall end, positioning it squarely with a carpenter's square.

◆ Cut a foot-long cleat and screw it on the underside of the top shelf flush with the back edge and the stringer end. Place the shelf on its side-wall cleat and screw the other cleat to the wall stringer so the top of the shelf fits against the tread above it.

◆ Mount the second shelf following the same procedure.

◆ Hang a plumb bob from a nail tacked to the front of the top shelf just beside the stringer and mark the front of the second shelf where the bob crosses it.

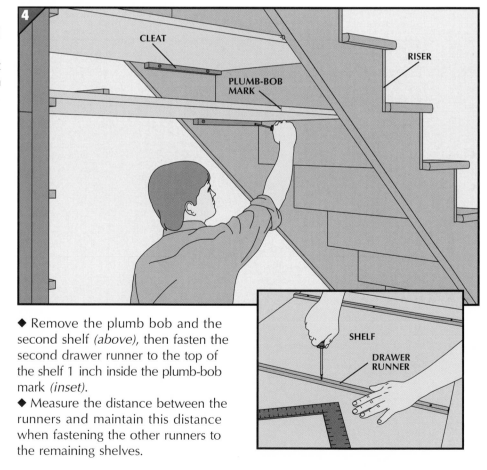

◆ Remove the plumb bob and the second shelf *(above)*, then fasten the second drawer runner to the top of the shelf 1 inch inside the plumb-bob mark *(inset)*.

◆ Measure the distance between the runners and maintain this distance when fastening the other runners to the remaining shelves.

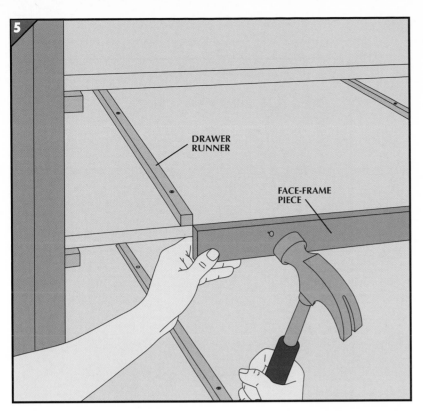

5. Starting the drawer facing.

◆ Measure along the front edge of the second shelf to determine the distance between the left-hand drawer runner and the stringer.

◆ Cut a 1-by-2 to this length as a face-frame piece and fasten it to the front edge of the shelf with a $1\frac{1}{2}$-inch finishing nail near each end *(left)*, aligning the top edge of the 1-by-2 with the top of the shelf.

◆ Fasten face-frame pieces to the remaining shelves in the same way, adding a third nail near the middle of the longer pieces.

◆ Cut 1-by-2 face-frame pieces to fit between the top of each shelf and the stringer, mitering the top end to fit flush against the stringer. Nail the pieces at the bottom to the right-hand drawer runner and toenail them at the top to the stringer.

6. Finishing the face frame.

◆ Cut 1-by-1 strips to fit along the bottom edge of the stringer as nailing surfaces for wallboard, mitering the ends to fit flush against the face-frame pieces, and nail them to the stringer.

◆ Complete the face frame by cutting a 1-by-2 to fit between the top shelf and the top of the subwall and nailing it to the shelves *(right)*.

◆ Build a drawer *(page 13)* for each shelf, making the false front $\frac{1}{2}$ inch larger all around.

◆ If you will be installing a light in the closet *(page 55)*, fasten the electrical box for the switch to one of the closet studs and the fixture box to the ceiling framing, then run the necessary wiring.

◆ Hang wallboard to finish the front wall of the closet and the shelf-drawer section *(pages 37-40)*.

◆ To conceal the cut edges of wallboard around the drawers, fasten strips of $\frac{1}{2}$- by $\frac{1}{2}$-inch edging to the face frame.

INSTALLING A FLAT-JAMB DOOR

1. Positioning the door.
◆ Cut out the soleplate at the bottom of the door opening *(page 37)*.
◆ With a helper, tilt the door into its opening, wedging the head jamb into position *(right)*, then swing the bottom into place.
◆ With a pry bar, gently remove the door stops from the door jambs. Doing so will enable you to fasten the jambs to the frame at the door-stop positions, then reinstall the stops to hide the nails.

2. Fastening the door jamb.
◆ At the top, bottom, and middle of the door, tap wood shims between each side jamb and the door frame, checking the unit for plumb with a carpenter's level as you work.
◆ Nail the jambs to the frame through the shims with 2-inch finishing nails *(left)*.
◆ Cut the shims flush with the jambs with a hand-saw and reinstall the door stops.

3. Installing door casing.
◆ Center the top casing over the opening, the lower edge flush with the bottom face of the head jamb, and fasten it to the jamb every 8 inches with 1-inch finishing nails.
◆ Nail the side pieces to the side jambs in the same way *(right)*, butting their mitered ends against those of the top piece, then lock the corners together by driving a $1\frac{1}{2}$-inch finishing nail through the edge of the side piece into the end of the top one.
◆ Sink the nailheads below the surface with a nail set and fill the holes with wood putty.

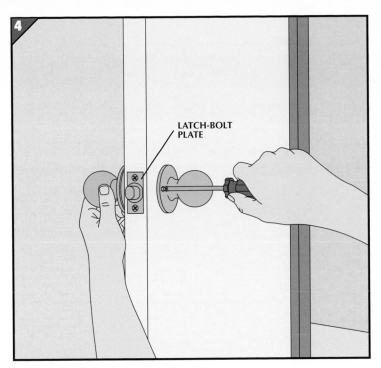

LATCH-BOLT PLATE

4. Installing the doorknob.

◆ Screw the strike plate into the precut mortise in the door jamb.

◆ Slip the latch-bolt assembly into its hole in the door edge so the beveled side of the bolt faces the direction in which the door closes, then screw the latch-bolt plate in place.

◆ Insert the shaft of the outside knob into the precut hole in the door and through the latch-bolt holes.

◆ Fit the inside knob assembly over the protruding shaft and fasten the units together with the screws provided *(left)*.

A CLOSET LIGHT

When you want to put a light fixture in a closet, the simplest method is to tap into power at a nearby electrical outlet and run cable to the light switch and fixture before you install wallboard. If you are experienced at working with wiring, you can do the job yourself. Check local electrical codes first for requirements.

The light fixture here hangs from a metal ceiling-fixture box nailed to the closet framing and the switch is installed in a flanged box nailed to a wall stud near the door. The fixture, switch, and outlet are joined with lengths of two-conductor 14-gauge NM cable and wired as shown in the insets. In this scheme, the white wire between the switch and the fixture is recoded black with paint or tape since it serves as a hot wire in a switch loop between the boxes.

⚠ **CAUTION** *Turn off the power to the circuit at the service panel before you connect the new cable at the existing outlet.*

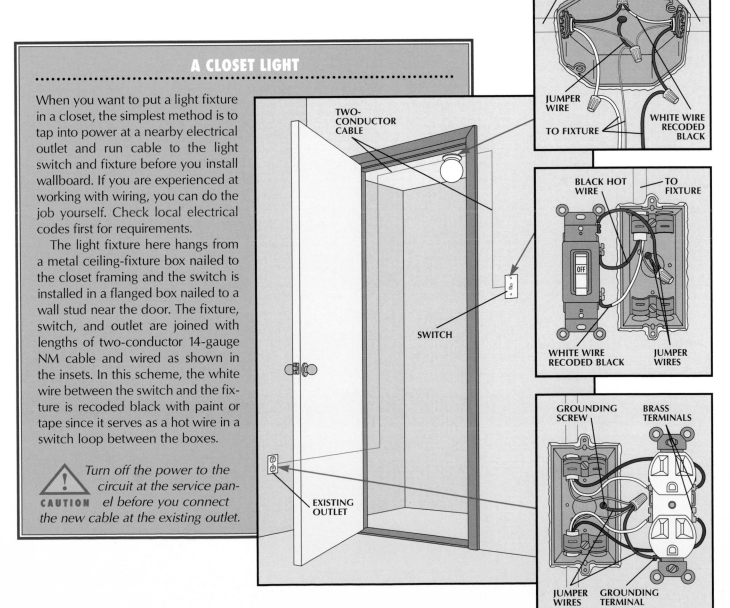

TWO-CONDUCTOR CABLE

SWITCH

EXISTING OUTLET

FROM OUTLET — TO SWITCH

JUMPER WIRE

TO FIXTURE

WHITE WIRE RECODED BLACK

BLACK HOT WIRE — TO FIXTURE

WHITE WIRE RECODED BLACK

JUMPER WIRES

GROUNDING SCREW — BRASS TERMINALS

JUMPER WIRES — GROUNDING TERMINAL

2 Organizing Living Areas and Bedrooms

To maximize space within a room, you can sometimes combine the functions of several pieces of furniture in one unit. The home-entertainment center, window-seat project, bunk bed/room divider, and Murphy bed illustrated in this chapter provide extra storage while occupying relatively small areas. You can also extend the available space in a room by recessing shelves into the gaps between wall studs.

Fastening a window seat to the wall →

A Home-Entertainment Center

The unit on these pages is configured to house the components of a typical home-entertainment system. Consisting of two modules fixed together with knockdown fasteners, it is simple to put together and can be disassembled quickly.

An Adaptable Design: The combination of fixed and adjustable shelves gives the structure rigidity as well as flexibility. A TV set can be placed on a fixed shelf, with movable shelves reserved for a VCR, stereo system, or other device; and the closed cabinet and drawers provide storage for video and cassette tapes, CDs, and related accessories.

 TOOLS

Tape measure	Electric drill	Hacksaw
Carpenter's	Hole saw (2")	Manual or power
square	Bar clamps	miter saw
Screwdriver	Table saw	Hex wrenches
	Circular saw	Router
	Saber saw	Nail set

 MATERIALS

Furniture-grade	Wood molding (2")	Power bar
plywood ($\frac{3}{4}$")	Shelf standards	Knockdown hard-
1 x 2s, 1 x 4s	Wood screws	ware connectors
Edge banding	($1\frac{1}{4}$" No. 8)	Door hinges
Hardboard ($\frac{1}{4}$")	Finishing nails (1")	Wood glue
	Drawer pulls	Wood putty
	Drawer glides	Felt pads

SAFETY TIPS

Wear goggles when you are using a hammer or power tool.

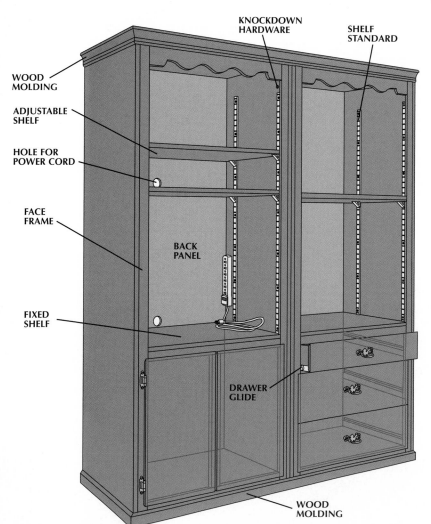

KNOCKDOWN HARDWARE

SHELF STANDARD

WOOD MOLDING

ADJUSTABLE SHELF

HOLE FOR POWER CORD

FACE FRAME

BACK PANEL

FIXED SHELF

DRAWER GLIDE

WOOD MOLDING

A home-entertainment center.

The home-entertainment center at left consists of two modules made of $\frac{3}{4}$-inch furniture-grade plywood, tied together with a pair of knock-down hardware connectors through the sides near the top and bottom. Modules 22 inches deep will accommodate a TV set of average size; but you can plan them to suit components of almost any dimensions. In each module, the top piece fits into rabbets *(page 10)* cut in the side pieces, while the bottom piece and a fixed shelf are held in dadoes *(page 11)* routed in the sides. A rabbet in the back edges of the side pieces forms a recess for the back panel, and dadoes routed vertically along the sides hold the standards for the adjustable shelves. An inset face frame adds rigidity to the structure. The drawers have false fronts and slide on commercial glides. Wood molding trims the top and bottom, and exposed edges of plywood are concealed with edge banding. To accommodate wiring for the various electronic components, a power bar is mounted to a side panel and holes for cords are drilled in the back.

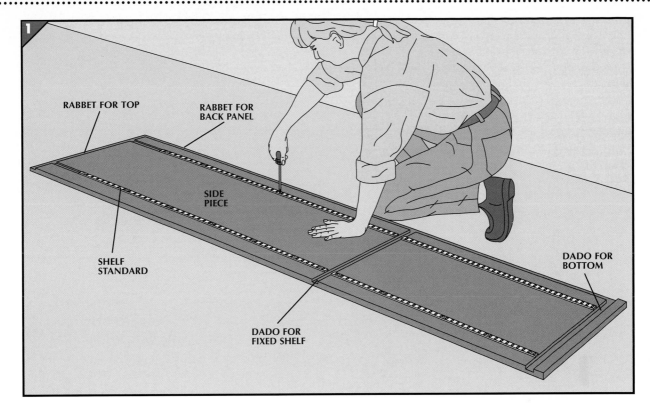

1

RABBET FOR TOP

RABBET FOR
BACK PANEL

SIDE
PIECE

SHELF
STANDARD

DADO FOR
BOTTOM

DADO FOR
FIXED SHELF

1. Preparing the pieces.

◆ Cut the side pieces for each module from $\frac{3}{4}$-inch furniture-grade plywood.

◆ Across the inner face of each piece, make the following $\frac{3}{4}$-inch-wide cuts with a router *(pages 10-11)*: a dado located $1\frac{1}{2}$ inches from the bottom to hold the bottom piece; a dado 29 inches from the bottom for the fixed shelf; and a rabbet along the top edge.

◆ Next, rout a dado the width of the shelf standards

4 inches from each edge, running from the rabbet at the top to the dado at the bottom.

◆ Finally, cut a 1-inch-wide rabbet along the back edge of each side to hold the back panel.

◆ With a hacksaw, trim four lengths of shelf standard *(page 21)*: two for the dadoes in the lower half of the sides and two for the top half.

◆ Screw the standards into the dadoes with the screws provided *(above)*.

TRICKS OF THE TRADE

Squaring the Modules

After securing a module with clamps *(Step 2)*, you can check whether the assembly is square by measuring it diagonally in both directions *(right)*. Identical diagonal measurements indicate that the module is positioned correctly. If it is not, loosen the clamps slightly and slide one jaw of each clamp outward at opposite corners, then tighten the clamps and measure the diagonals again.

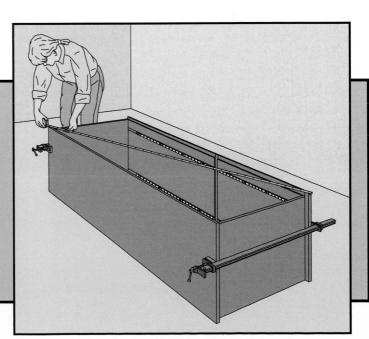

2. Assembling the modules.

◆ For the top, bottom, and fixed shelf, cut three pieces of plywood of identical size: Make them $\frac{3}{4}$ inch narrower than the desired total width of each module and 1 inch shallower than the depth.

◆ Cut a $\frac{3}{4}$-inch-deep $1\frac{1}{2}$-inch-wide notch at the front corners of the fixed shelf to accommodate the face frame (Step 3).

◆ Spread wood glue in the dadoes and rabbets of the side pieces. Have a helper stand the sides on their front edges, then fit the top and bottom pieces into place.

◆ Slide the fixed shelf in its dado, then fasten the top, bottom, and shelf to the sides, driving two $1\frac{1}{4}$-inch No. 8 wood screws into each joint (right).

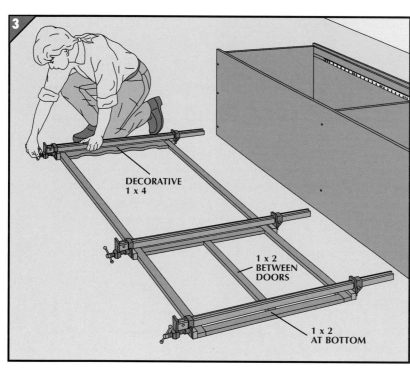

DECORATIVE 1 x 4

1 x 2 BETWEEN DOORS

1 x 2 AT BOTTOM

3. Building the face frames.

For each module, make a face frame that sits against the inner surfaces of the sides, top, and bottom, and in the notches cut in the front corners of the fixed shelf.

◆ Measure the distance between the inner surfaces of the top and bottom pieces, and cut two 1-by-2s for the sides of the frame.

◆ For the horizontal sections of the frame, trim two more 1-by-2s to fit between the sides of the frame at the bottom and at the fixed shelf, then cut a 1-by-4 to this length for the top of the frame. If desired, scroll a decorative pattern along one edge with a saber saw.

◆ To frame the door section, cut a 1-by-2 to fit vertically between the bottom and fixed-shelf pieces.

◆ Apply wood glue to the ends and edges of the pieces that will be joined, then clamp the pieces together (left) until the glue cures.

4. Attaching the back panels and face frames.

◆ Trim a piece of $\frac{1}{4}$-inch hardboard to fit flush with the top and bottom of the unit and in the rabbets in the sides.

◆ With the module still lying face-down, position the back panel on the unit and fasten it to the sides, top, bottom, and fixed shelf with 1-inch finishing nails driven at each corner and every 6 inches in between (right).

◆ With a helper, turn the module onto its back and set the face frame in place so its front edges are flush with those of the unit. Nail the frame to the top, bottom, and fixed shelf.

◆ Cut the adjustable shelves from $\frac{3}{4}$-inch plywood to fit between the sides and add edge banding (page 12) to exposed edges.

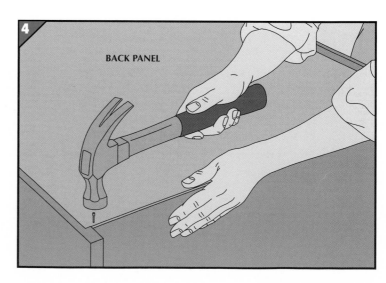

BACK PANEL

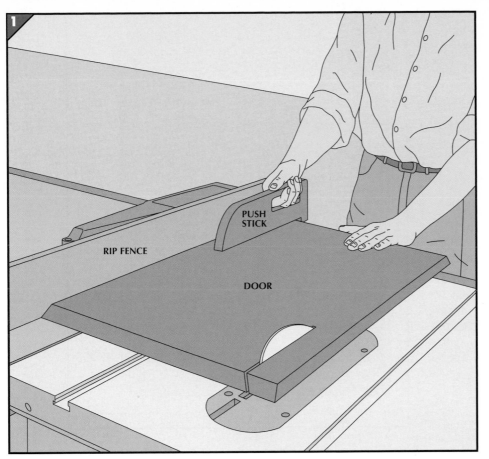

1. Beveling the doors.

◆ Outline each door on the inside face of a piece of $\frac{3}{4}$-inch plywood, sizing the door $\frac{1}{2}$ inch larger all around than its face-frame opening in the module.

◆ Angle the blade of a table saw to 30 degrees, place the piece outside-face down on the table, and align the cutting line for the top or bottom of the door with the blade.

◆ Butt the rip fence against the piece and lock the fence in place.

◆ With your left hand on the panel midway between the blade and the fence to keep the workpiece pressed lightly against the fence, advance the board with a push stick in your right hand, beveling one end.

◆ Bevel the opposite end and both sides in the same way *(left)*. *(In the illustration, the blade guard has been removed for clarity.)*

2. Hanging the doors.

◆ Mark hinge positions on the inside face of each door on one edge, one-quarter of the way from the top and bottom ends.

◆ At each mark, position a 30-degree-bevel semiconcealed door hinge against the door so its beveled flange *(photograph)* is flush against the door edge.

◆ Fasten the hinges to the door with the screws provided *(right)*.

◆ Fasten felt pads to the door's inside face near the top and bottom along the opposite edge.

◆ Hang the doors on the module as for a kneewall closet *(page 49, Step 4)*.

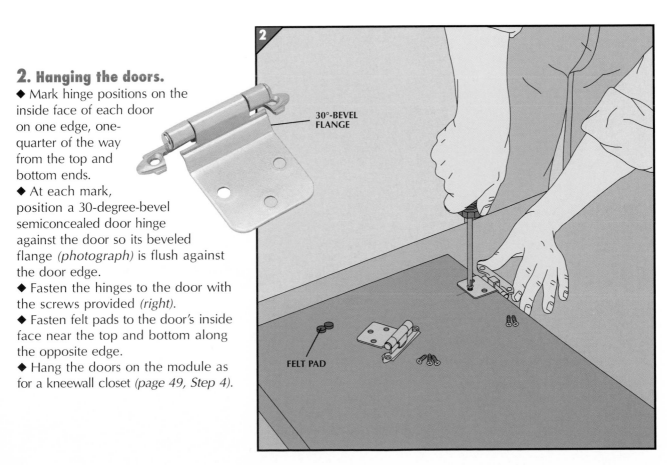

MOUNTING DRAWERS

1. Planning the installation.

◆ Determine the number of drawers you want in the module, their sizes, and the height of their false fronts, taking into account any units that will serve a specific purpose such as holding compact discs *(opposite)* or tapes. Size each false front so it extends $\frac{1}{4}$ inch below the bottom of the drawer and 1 inch on each side. In addition, leave a $\frac{1}{8}$-inch gap between the fronts.

◆ To mark the positions of the drawer glides on the module sides, start with the bottom drawer: Separate a drawer glide *(opposite, Step 3)* into its two pieces and measure the distance from the lower edge of the glide to the screw holes, add $\frac{1}{4}$ inch, and draw a line that distance above the cabinet bottom on the inner edges of the face frame.

◆ For the second drawer, measure the height of the bottom drawer's false front and subtract $\frac{1}{2}$ inch. Draw a line that distance above the first line.

◆ To mark the glide position for the remaining drawers, measure the height of the false front directly below and add $\frac{1}{8}$ inch.

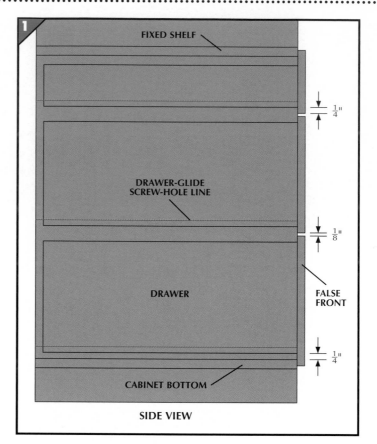

SIDE VIEW

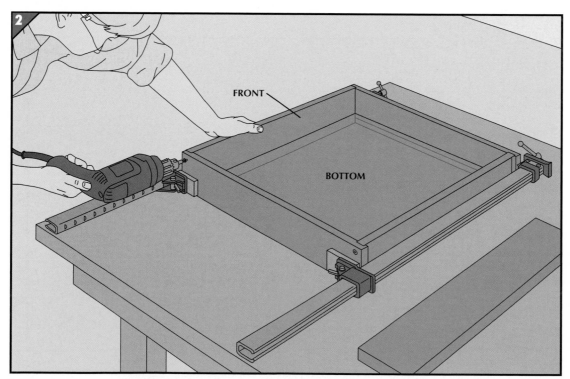

2. Making the drawers.

◆ Build the drawers *(page 13, Step 1)*, sizing the components according to your plan in Step 1 and fastening them together with $1\frac{1}{4}$-inch No. 8 wood screws *(above)*.

If you are making a CD drawer *(opposite)*, prepare the sides and dividers before putting the unit together.

◆ Attach the false fronts to the drawers *(page 13, Step 2)*.

One or more drawers of a home-entertainment center can be outfitted to hold a CD collection. Size the drawers to be slightly deeper than the height of a CD jewel box—about 5 inches. When cutting the parts, make $\frac{3}{4}$-inch plywood dividers to fit between the front and back. Before assembling the drawer, clamp one side and one divider edge-to-edge with the front ends aligned, and rout a series of $\frac{1}{2}$-inch-wide dadoes, separated by $\frac{1}{2}$ inch of solid wood, across both pieces. Repeat the cuts on the other side and divider, and on any dividers for the center of the drawer. Assemble the drawer (*opposite, Step 2*), placing the dividers about 6 inches apart and fastening them to the front and back pieces with $1\frac{1}{4}$-inch No. 8 wood screws, then attach the false front.

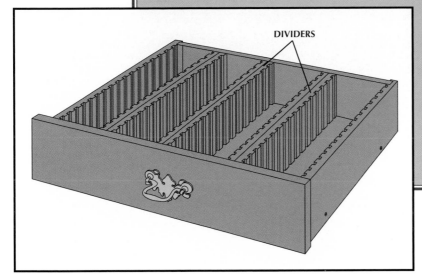

DIVIDERS

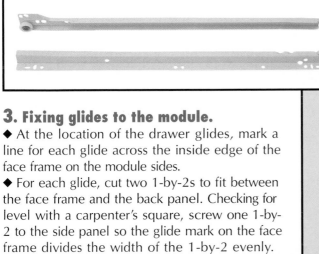

3. Fixing glides to the module.
◆ At the location of the drawer glides, mark a line for each glide across the inside edge of the face frame on the module sides.
◆ For each glide, cut two 1-by-2s to fit between the face frame and the back panel. Checking for level with a carpenter's square, screw one 1-by-2 to the side panel so the glide mark on the face frame divides the width of the 1-by-2 evenly. Fasten the second 1-by-2 to the first to form a cleat that will enable you to mount the drawer glide flush with the face frame.
◆ Separate all the drawer glides (*photograph*) into pieces and set one that attaches to the module against the cleat so the screw holes are centered on the marked line. Fasten it with the screws provided (*right*).
◆ Screw the remaining glides to the module in the same way.

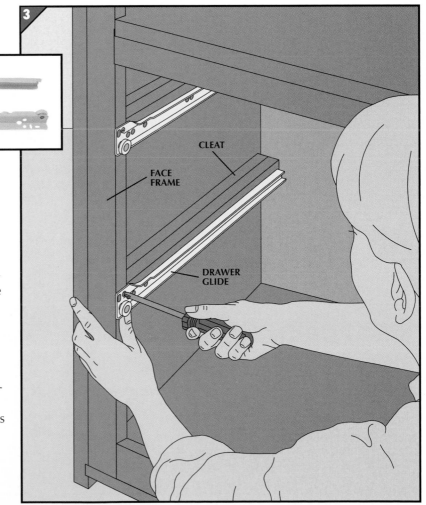

CLEAT

FACE FRAME

DRAWER GLIDE

4. Fitting glides on the drawers.

◆ Position the drawer glide on the drawer according to the manufacturer's instructions; for the model shown, the channel is set flush with the front of the drawer with the roller at the back.

◆ Fasten the glide to the drawer through the oblong screw holes *(right)*.

◆ Test-fit the drawer in the module; it should slide smoothly. If not, loosen the screws and move the channel sideways slightly.

◆ When the glides are well adjusted, drive screws through the remaining holes.

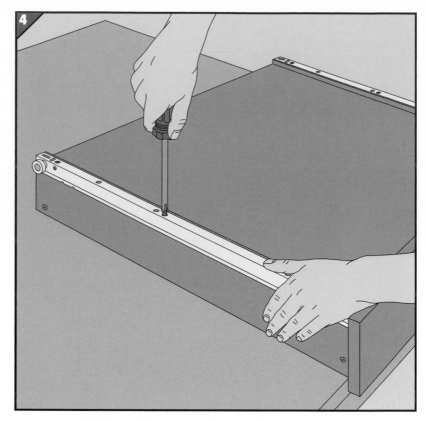

5. Attaching the drawer pulls.

For a single-fastener drawer pull, attach it as described on page 13, Step 2.

◆ For a two-fastener pull, measure the distance between its two screw holes, divide the measurement by two, and mark this distance on each side of the center of the false front *(left)*.

◆ Drill a clearance hole into the false front and through the drawer front at each mark for the screws provided with the drawer pull.

◆ Holding the drawer pull in position against the false front, drive the screws from the inside to fasten the pull to the drawer *(inset)*.

TYING THE UNITS TOGETHER

1. Joining the modules.

◆ With a helper, move the modules to their final location and place them side by side.

◆ Mark points on one side panel near the top and bottom 1 inch from the front.

◆ At each mark, drill a clearance hole for knockdown fasteners *(photograph)* through the sides. This type of fastener consists of a bolt and a flanged nut; size the hole to accommodate the nut.

◆ Slip a matching bolt and nut into opposite sides of each hole, then tighten them with two hex wrenches, holding the nut steady with one and turning the bolt with the other. When one of the pieces bites into the wood, finish tightening the other *(right)*.

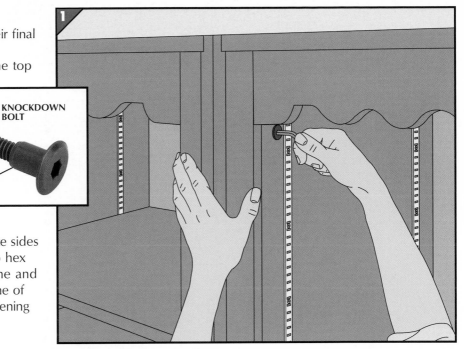

KNOCKDOWN BOLT

FLANGED NUT

WOOD MOLDING

DECORATIVE TOP

2. Adding a decorative top.

◆ Trim a piece of $\frac{3}{4}$-inch plywood $\frac{1}{16}$ inch larger all around than the combined length and width of the units.

◆ Cut three lengths of 2-inch-wide wood molding to fit around the front and sides of the decorative top, mitering both ends of the front piece and one end of the side pieces at 45-degree angles.

◆ Fasten the molding to the edges of the top with 1-inch finishing nails at 6-inch intervals so the top edge of the trim is flush with the surface of the top and the miters fit together tightly.

◆ Sink the nailheads with a nail set and cover the holes with wood putty.

◆ With a helper, lift the top into position on the modules *(left)*.

◆ Attach the top to the modules, driving a $1\frac{1}{4}$-inch No. 8 wood screw through the module top panels into the decorative top at each corner.

◆ Cut and miter molding for the bottom of the modules, then nail the front piece to the bottom panels and the side pieces to the side panels.

ACCOMMODATING WIRES

1. Drilling holes.

◆ Mark a point in the back panel about 2 inches up from the fixed shelf that will house a TV set.

◆ Fit an electric drill with a 2-inch hole saw and drill through the back panel at the point *(right)*.

◆ Drill a hole in the same manner above any shelf that will hold an electronic component.

◆ If you will be running wires between the modules, drill holes at the appropriate locations in the adjoining sides of the modules.

FIXED
SHELF

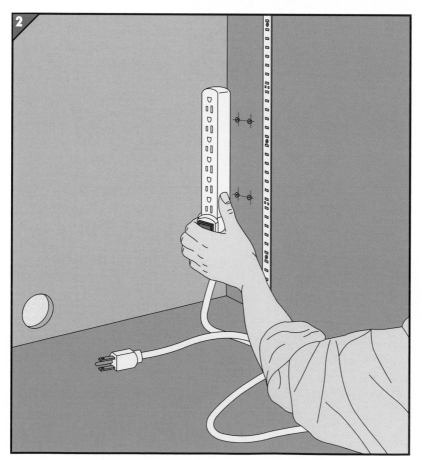

2. Mounting a power bar.

◆ Measure the relative positions of the mounting holes on the back of the power bar and transfer the measurements to the inside of one module side panel near the back.

◆ Drive a screw supplied with the power bar into the panel at each mark, leaving the heads protruding about $\frac{1}{8}$ inch.

◆ Hook the power bar on the screws *(left)*, then tug down on the bar to secure it.

◆ Run the power bar's cord through the drilled hole in the back panel and plug it into the nearest outlet.

A Window Seat with Storage

The combination of bookcases, side tables, and window seat provides ample space for storing and displaying a wide variety of items, as well as a bright, comfortable place to sit and relax. The elements can be arranged in a variety of ways *(opposite)*.

The side tables and bookcases are built in almost the same manner as the stackable shelf boxes on pages 10 to 12. The only differences are that they are larger and lack back panels, but have fixed shelves for added stability.

TOOLS

Electronic stud finder	Bar clamps
Circular saw	Screwdriver
Electric drill	Carpenter's Square
Hacksaw	

MATERIALS

Furniture-grade plywood ($\frac{3}{4}$")	Piano hinge
Wood screws ($1\frac{1}{4}$" No. 8)	Lid support
	Wood glue

SAFETY TIPS

Protect your eyes with goggles when you are operating a power tool.

Seating with storage.

The centerpiece of this storage system is a simple four-sided seat box, 18 inches deep, made of $\frac{3}{4}$-inch furniture-grade plywood. It is held in place by a three-piece plinth fastened to the floor. The sides of the box fit in rabbets cut in the ends of the front panel, and the bottom panel is held in dadoes cut in the front and side pieces. The lid of the seat is hinged to a strap screwed to a T-shaped back rail, and has a mechanism that can lock it in the open position. Framing the seat are stacking shelf boxes *(pages 10-12)* with fixed shelves *(page 22, Step 2)* but no back panels, built the same depth as the seat box and placed on plinths. Flanking the boxes are wide side tables of similar design. The side tables and the shelf boxes at the top of each stack are finished with decorative caps.

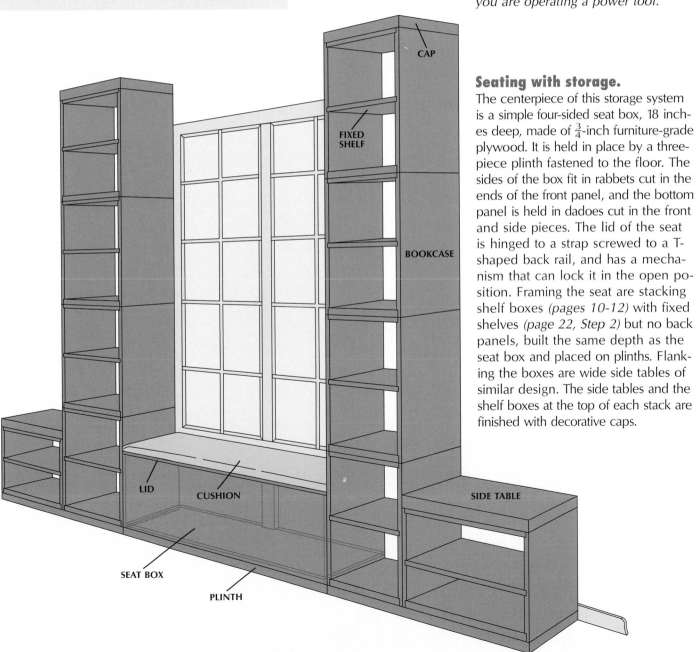

ALTERNATIVE ARRANGEMENTS

Framing a window with boxes.
The flexible construction of stackable shelf boxes *(pages 10-12)* makes it easy to adapt a storage system around a window to suit your needs. Both arrangements shown below share a seat box centered under the window. The one at left has two pairs of shelf boxes flanking the seat, with a capped top joining the boxes. Four boxes made with back panels are fastened to the wall *(page 14)* above the window. The setup at right has a single side table placed to one side of the seat and a stack of tables on the other side. The module at the bottom of the stack is as tall as the seat; the others are each built 6 inches taller.

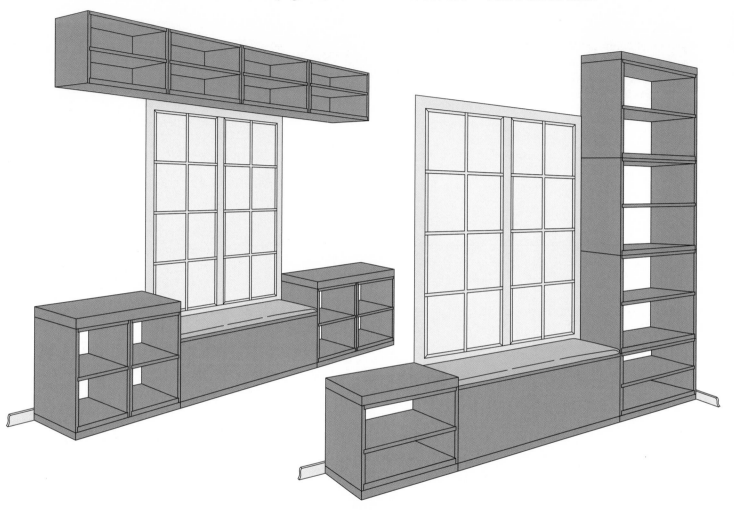

FASTENING THE PLINTH

1. Building the plinth.
◆ From three lengths of $\frac{3}{4}$-inch plywood cut 2 inches wide, make the plinth with the front strip as long as the window's width and the side pieces $17\frac{1}{4}$ inches long.
◆ Join the side pieces to the front in a U with four $1\frac{1}{4}$-inch No. 8 wood screws.
◆ Cut two triangular pieces of plywood so the sides are 3 to 4 inches long and screw them to the inside corners of the plinth, flush with the plinth top.
◆ Remove baseboard from the wall under the window, then position the assembly on the floor with the sides aligned with the window's side casing, counterbore a screw hole halfway through the edges every 12 inches, and screw the plinth to the floor *(right)*.

PLINTH

BUILDING THE SEAT BOX

1. Assembling the box.

◆ Cut the front of the box to size and rout a $\frac{3}{4}$-inch-wide rabbet *(page 10)* along each end of it, then make side pieces to fit into the rabbets.

◆ Rout dadoes $\frac{1}{4}$ inch from the bottoms of the front and sides, and cut a bottom panel to fit in the dadoes.

◆ Fasten the sides in the rabbets with two screws at each joint, then turn the assembly on one side. Slide the bottom panel into its dadoes and secure it there with three screws in each side.

◆ For the back rail, cut a 3-inch-wide strip of plywood to fit between the sides at the top and bottom, and attach it to the sides with two screws at each end *(right)*.

◆ Make the vertical support at the back from another 3-inch-wide strip of plywood, and screw it to the bottom panel and to the back rail with two counterbored screws at each end.

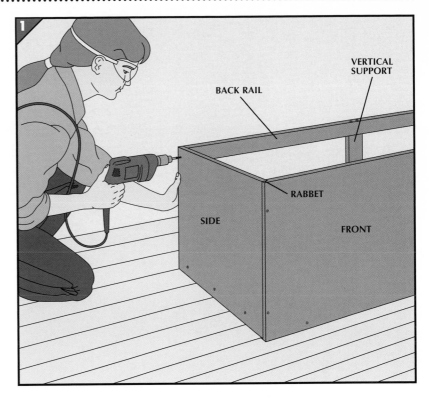

2. Attaching the lid.

◆ Cut a lid to the length of the box, but 2 inches shorter than its depth, then make a hinge strap as long as the box from a 2-inch-wide plywood strip.

◆ With a hacksaw, trim a piano hinge to fit the lid, then hinge one edge of the strap to the lid *(page 15, Step 1)*.

◆ Set the lid on the box so the back edge of the strap is flush with the outer side of the back rail, and secure it there with two bar clamps. Fasten the lid to the back rail, driving a screw every 12 inches *(above)*.

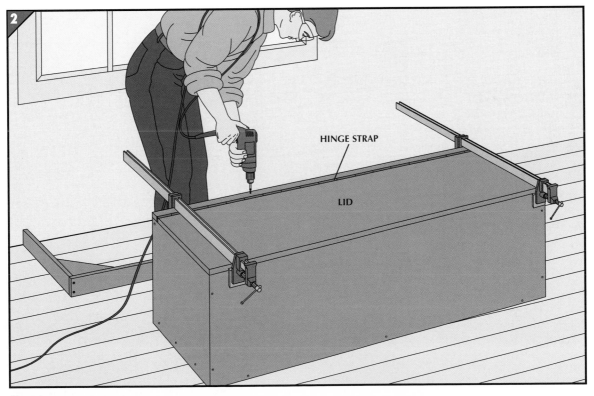

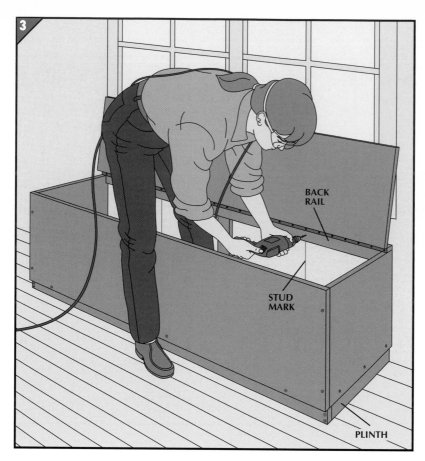

3. Fixing the box to the wall.

◆ With an electronic stud finder, locate and mark the stud positions on the wall under the window.

◆ Center the seat box on the plinth and attach it to the wall by driving a screw through the back rail at each stud mark *(left)*.

4. Installing a lid support.

◆ Position a lid support with one flange on the underside of the lid and, for the side-mounting model shown, the other on the inside of the side panel. Mark the screw holes.

◆ Drill pilot holes for the screws provided at the marks, then fasten the support to the box *(right)*. The support will lock the lid in place when opened, keeping it from slamming shut.

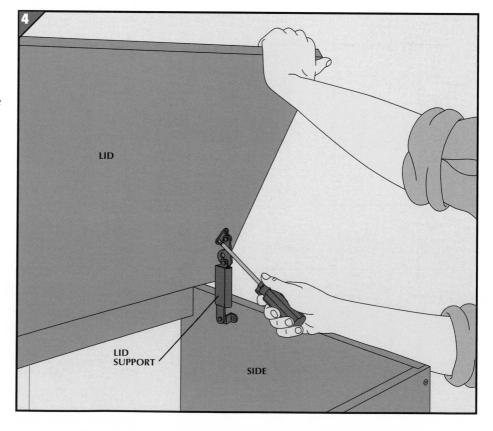

CAPPING THE SHELF BOXES AND SIDE TABLES

1. Making the caps.

◆ Build shelf boxes and side tables *(pages 10-12)* of a size and quantity to suit your needs and rabbeting the top edges so they can be stacked. Stack them on each side of the window as desired, securing the bottom modules to the floor with plinths.

◆ For each box or table at the top of a stack, cut a decorative cap to the same dimensions as the box. Also cut 2-inch-wide front, back, and side pieces to fit the outer edges of the cap.

◆ Position the pieces face-down on a worktable, apply wood glue on the inside faces of the sides, front, and back along the points where they will contact the cap *(right)*, and secure the assembly together with two bar clamps so the top edges of the strips are flush with the top face of the cap. Check all the corners for square with a carpenter's square.

◆ Once the glue is dry, remove the clamps and fit the cap in the rabbets routed around the top of the unit.

TRICKS OF THE TRADE

Securing a Seat Cushion

To keep window-seat cushions from sliding off when the top is opened, apply strips of hook-and-loop fastener tape (often known by its trade name, Velcro) to the lid and cushion. Cut two 15-inch lengths of the fastener, peel off the backing, and stick them on the lid in an L shape near each corner *(right)*; then cut two identical lengths and press them in place on the bottom of the cushion. If the fasteners are not self-adhesive, glue the strips to the lid and sew them to the cushion.

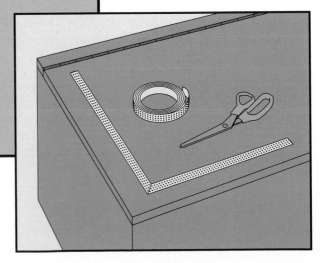

Mounting Shelves Between Studs

Most houses have interior walls framed with studs. By opening up these walls, you can make room for shallow shelves to display curios and decorative items. In a kitchen, you can store spices and other cooking necessities in the space.

Getting Ready: Before cutting into a wall, locate and mark stud positions. Modern houses generally have 2-by-4s placed 16 inches on center. This arrangement yields an area between studs $14\frac{1}{2}$ inches wide and $3\frac{1}{2}$ inches deep—excluding the thickness of the wall covering. An older house, though, may have wider or irregularly sized cavities.

Determine that the part of the wall you have chosen does not contain plumbing pipes or wiring. If the space seems clear, cut an exploratory opening just large enough to see into or to probe for obstacles. If you encounter utilities, seal the opening and try again in another area.

Breaking into the Wall: Cut through wallboard with a saber saw. For plaster, make a small hole with a cold chisel to determine whether there is wood or metal lath behind it, then fit the saw with a blade appropriate for the material.

 When opening walls, take precautions against releasing lead and asbestos particles (page 45).

 TOOLS

Electronic stud finder
Tape measure
Electric drill
Saber saw
Hammer
Carpenter's level
Table saw

 **MATERIALS**

1 x 2s
Finishing nails ($1\frac{1}{2}$")
Wood glue
Furniture-grade
    plywood ($\frac{1}{4}$", $\frac{1}{2}$")
Panel adhesive
Wood trim

 SAFETY TIPS

When you are operating a power tool or hammering, wear goggles to prevent eye injury.

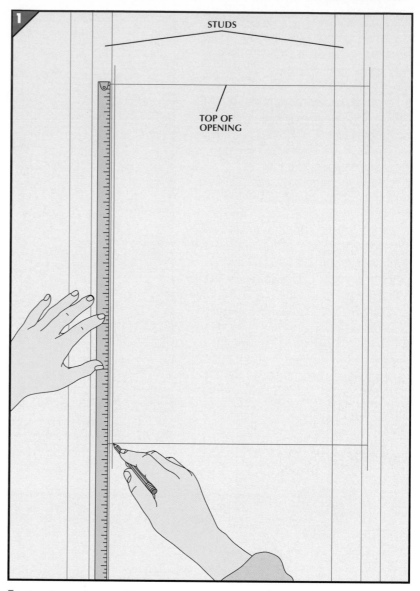

1. Cutting the wall opening.

◆ Locate the studs adjoining the proposed opening *(page 14, Step 1)*, then outline the opening's top and bottom with a pencil and tape measure; consider the number of shelves, the space between them, and their thickness when calculating the opening's height. Mark the sides along the inside edges of the studs *(above)*, forming a rectangle. Use a level to ensure that the top and bottom lines are horizontal.

◆ With a drill and a spade bit slightly larger than the saber-saw blade you will be using to cut the opening, bore a hole through the wall just inside each corner of the rectangle.

◆ Starting at one of the upper holes, saw away the wallboard within the rectangle.

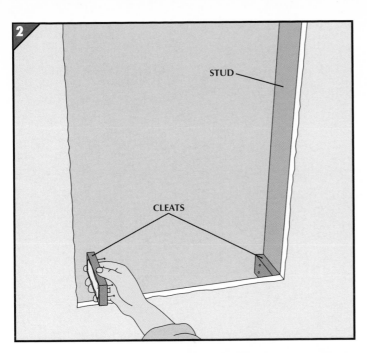

2. Putting in shelf cleats.

◆ Measure the depth of the studs adjoining the opening and cut two 1-by-2 strips to this measurement to serve as cleats.

◆ Drive two $1\frac{1}{2}$-inch finishing nails into the cleats near each end so the nail tips just appear on the opposite side.

◆ Apply wood glue to each cleat, then position them across the studs so the top of each is flush with the bottom edge of the opening and one end sits against the back of the wallboard *(right)*.

◆ Check with a carpenter's level that the cleats are horizontal, then drive the nails into the studs.

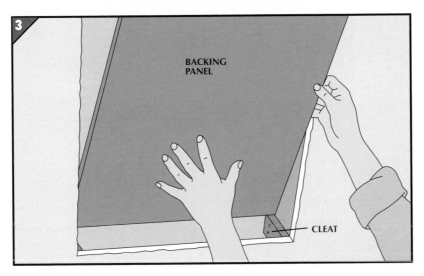

3. Backing the opening.

◆ Measure the opening's dimensions and cut a piece of $\frac{1}{4}$-inch furniture-grade plywood to fit snugly against the wall at the back.

◆ Coat the back of the plywood with panel adhesive and, resting the bottom of the panel on the cleats *(left)*, push it firmly into place against the wall.

4. Putting in the shelves.

◆ Measure the width of the opening and cut the desired number of shelves, plus one, to this dimension from $\frac{1}{2}$-inch plywood; make the width of the shelves equal to the depth of the opening, including the wallboard thickness.

◆ Fasten the bottom shelf to the cleats with two nails at each end.

◆ For each subsequent shelf, cut two supports from $\frac{1}{2}$-inch plywood equal in width to the shelves and equal in length to the desired space between shelves.

◆ Glue and nail the first two supports to the studs as you did the cleats, resting them on the bottom shelf.

◆ Nail the second shelf to the top ends of the supports.

◆ Install the remaining supports *(right)* and shelves in the same way.

◆ To close off the top of the opening, fasten the extra shelf to the uppermost supports before installing them.

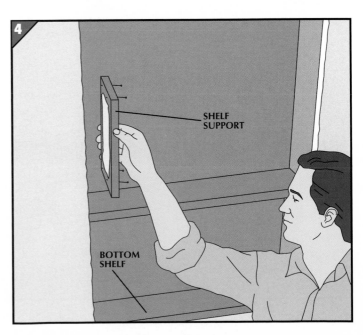

5. Trimming the opening.

◆ Cut two strips of molding as long as the height of the opening, less $\frac{1}{2}$ inch.

◆ Apply wood glue on the back of one strip and position it along one side of the opening, aligning its inner edge with the inside face of the shelf supports and its bottom end with the middle of the bottom shelf. Fasten the strip in place, driving a nail near each end and every 6 inches in between.

◆ Attach the second strip along the opposite side of the opening in the same way.

◆ Cut two more trim strips for the top and bottom, then attach them *(right)*, driving the nails into the top and bottom shelves.

◆ Cover the exposed edges of the shelves with edge banding *(page 12)*, if desired.

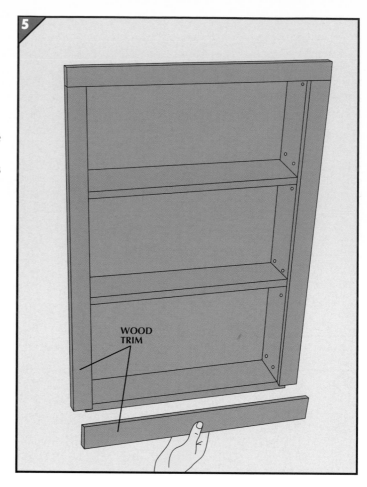

WOOD TRIM

A WALL OF RECESSED SHELVES

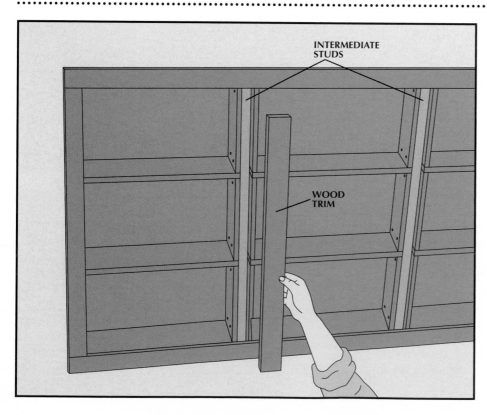

INTERMEDIATE STUDS

WOOD TRIM

Expanding the opening.

◆ If you want to install a number of shelves along one wall, cut all the openings between adjacent studs, then remove the wallboard from the outer edge of intermediate studs.

◆ Install cleats, a back panel, and shelves in each opening, then fasten trim along the outside, top, and bottom of the extended opening.

◆ For each intermediate stud, cut a trim strip wide enough to cover the studs and edges of the adjoining shelf supports, and long enough to fit between the top and bottom trim pieces *(left)*. Nail the trim to the studs.

VARIATIONS ON IN-THE-WALL SHELVING

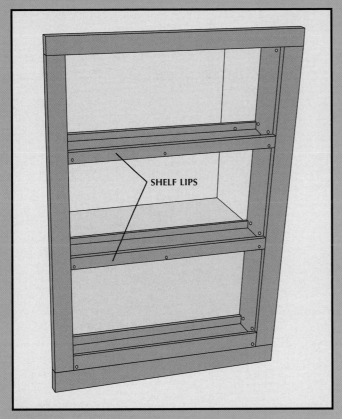

SHELF LIPS

With only minor modifications to the techniques on pages 72 to 74, you can create variations on the shelving system. In the case of most interior walls, you can make the shelves accessible from both sides. Cut the wall opening on one side, then drill a hole through the second side from inside the opening at each corner. Use the holes as guides in cutting away the wallboard from the second side.

Put in shelf cleats, but no back panel. Cut the shelves $\frac{1}{2}$ inch narrower than the depth of the opening and fasten them so the edges are inset from each side of the wall by $\frac{1}{4}$ inch. Then, for each shelf, cut two $\frac{1}{4}$- by 1-inch lips to fit between the shelf supports and fasten them to both edges of each shelf with $\frac{1}{2}$-inch finishing nails so their bottom edges are flush with the undersides of the shelves *(left)*. The lips will prevent items from slipping off the shelving. Then, trim the sides and top of the opening.

To display decorative objects, you may prefer glass shelves to wooden ones. Cut the opening from one side of the wall, then put in cleats and a back panel. Instead of nailing shelf supports to the studs adjoining the opening, fasten $\frac{1}{4}$-inch-thick wood strips equal in length to the height of the opening and as wide as the shelves. Have the shelves cut from $\frac{3}{8}$-inch-thick glass—which is thick enough to resist impact—but make them slightly shorter than the width of the opening to accommodate support clips *(inset)*.

Fit an electric drill with a bit the size of the pins of the shelf clips. At each desired shelf position, drill two level holes through the trim and into each stud. Slip a shelf clip into each hole, align the slots horizontally, then mount the shelves in the clips *(right)*.

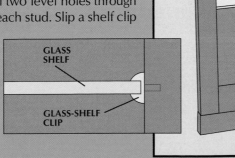

GLASS SHELF

GLASS-SHELF CLIP

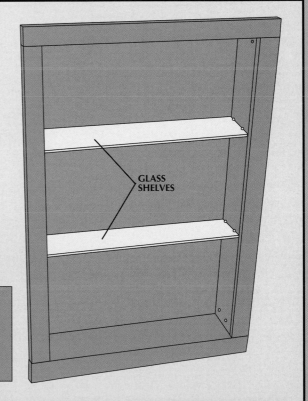

GLASS SHELVES

A Bunk Bed/Room Divider

The combination of bunk beds and storage units offers an imaginative solution to the space problems created when two youngsters share one room. Built to reach the ceiling, with the bunks opening on opposite sides, the project functions as a room partition that occupies less floor space than two single beds and gives each child a private living and storage area.

Planning: The unit on these pages is sized to reach an 8-foot ceiling and to hold a standard 39- by 75-inch mattress. If you build yours to this height, be sure there is ample ventilation, heat, and light on both sides; or, decrease the height by eliminating the cabinet units and lowering the bunk-bed section by 16 inches. You can change the width of the beds to accommodate special-size mattresses, but corresponding changes in the dimensions of other sections will be necessary as well.

As you cut the parts, measure and saw one piece at a time; otherwise, the kerf lost in cutting will affect later measurements. Because the bed section is so large, assemble it in the room it is to occupy. The other sections can be put together elsewhere, then moved into the room and screwed to the bunk beds.

Anatomy of a bunk bed/room divider.

Each component of this project—bunks, bookcase-closets, cabinets, and ladder—is constructed separately, and can be arranged as shown in the front and back views below or in other combinations. The bookcase-closet units with cabinets on top are placed at one end of the bunks, which incorporate three low drawers. A drop-leaf desk with fold-in braces is hinged to a fixed shelf set in a dado cut in the side pieces of the bookcase; the other shelves are adjustable. All major parts of the project are made of $\frac{3}{4}$-inch furniture-grade plywood, which can be finished with a satin oil to bring out the natural beauty of the wood. If you prefer to paint the unit, you can economize by using a less expensive grade of $\frac{3}{4}$-inch plywood. The exposed edges are concealed with edge banding.

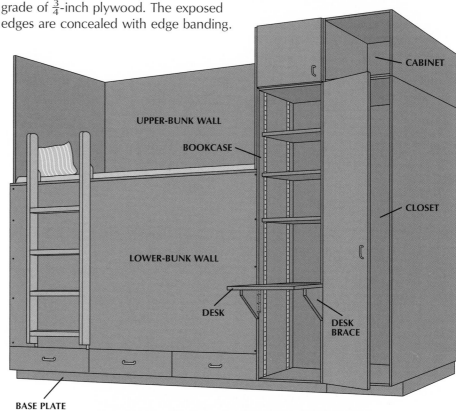

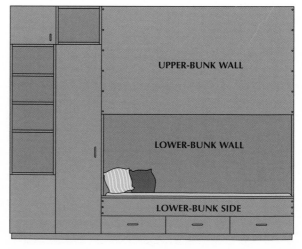

BACK VIEW

76

Circular saw or
table saw
Saber saw or
backsaw
Hacksaw
Carpenter's square
Combination square
Tape measure

C-clamps
Corner clamps
Handscrew clamps
Bar or pipe clamps
Hammer
Router
Electric drill
Screwdriver
Awl

MATERIALS

Furniture-grade
plywood ($\frac{3}{4}$")
2 x 2s, 1 x 4s, 1 x 6s
Wood trim ($\frac{3}{4}$" x $\frac{3}{4}$")
Edge banding
Drawer glides
Shelf standards
Door hinges
Piano hinge

Magnetic catches
Wood screws ($\frac{5}{8}$" No. 6,
 $1\frac{1}{4}$", $1\frac{1}{2}$", 2" No. 10)
Washers (No. 10)
Drawer and door pulls
Finishing nails ($1\frac{1}{2}$")
Wood glue
Masking tape
Sandpaper
 (medium grade)

SAFETY TIPS

*Wear goggles when you
are operating a power
tool or hammering nails.*

CONSTRUCTING THE BED SECTION

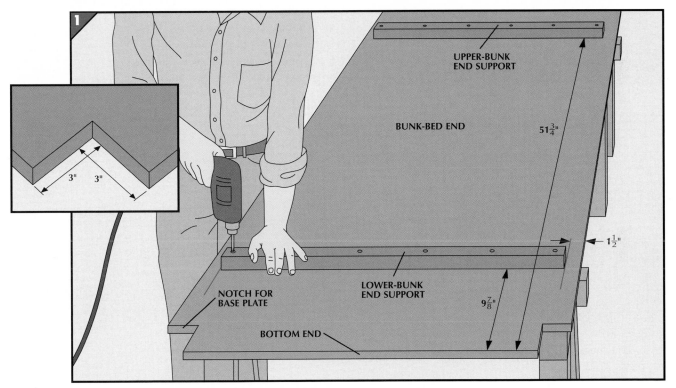

1. Preparing the bunk-bed ends.

◆ With a circular saw or table saw, cut the two bunk ends to width (41 inches) from two sheets of $\frac{3}{4}$-inch plywood. Set the waste pieces aside as false fronts for the drawers *(Step 12)*.

◆ To make space for the recessed base plate, cut 3-inch-square notches at the bottom corners of the bunk ends with a saber saw or backsaw *(inset)*.

◆ Cut two 2-by-2s 38 inches long as horizontal supports for the ends of the bunk bottoms, spread wood glue on one side of each piece, and position them $9\frac{7}{8}$ and $51\frac{3}{4}$ inches from the bottom of the bunk end and $1\frac{1}{2}$ inches from the edges.

◆ Check with a carpenter's square that the supports are perpendicular to the edges of the bunk end, then fasten them in place with 2-inch No. 10 wood screws driven near each end and at 7-inch intervals in between *(above)*.

◆ Prepare the other bunk end in the same way.

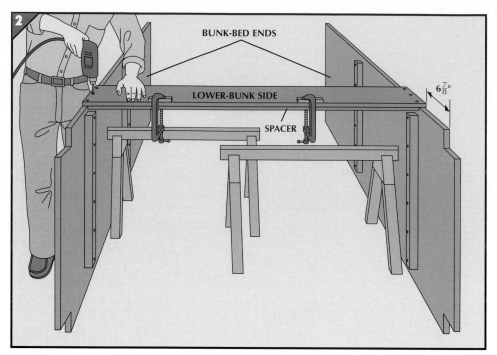

2. Attaching the lower-bunk side.

◆ Cut the lower-bunk side $6\frac{1}{4}$- by $78\frac{3}{8}$-inches from $\frac{3}{4}$-inch plywood.

◆ Cut another piece 3- by $76\frac{7}{8}$-inches as a spacer and, protecting its surface with wood pads, clamp it to the back of the lower-bunk side along an edge so it is $\frac{3}{4}$ inch from each end of the side piece.

◆ Set the bunk-bed ends on edge with the bunk-end supports facing inward;

use two sawhorses to prop up the ends.

◆ Position the lower-bunk side across the bunk ends with one edge $6\frac{7}{8}$ inches above the base-plate notches, then butt the bunk ends against the spacer.

◆ Drill three countersunk pilot holes for $1\frac{1}{2}$-inch No. 10 wood screws and washers through the lower-bunk side into each bunk end, then place the washers and drive the screws (above).

3. Fastening the upper-bunk wall to the bunk-bed ends.

◆ Cut the upper-bunk wall $44\frac{1}{4}$- by $78\frac{3}{8}$-inches from $\frac{3}{4}$-inch plywood, then clamp the spacer used in Step 2 along its bottom edge.

◆ Position the wall across the bunk ends so its top edge is flush with the upper corners of the ends; butt the bunk ends against the spacer, then secure the corners formed by the wall and ends with a pair of corner clamps.

◆ Fasten the wall to the bunk ends as you did the lower-bunk side (Step 2), driving a countersunk screw and washer at each corner and at 7-inch intervals in between (right).

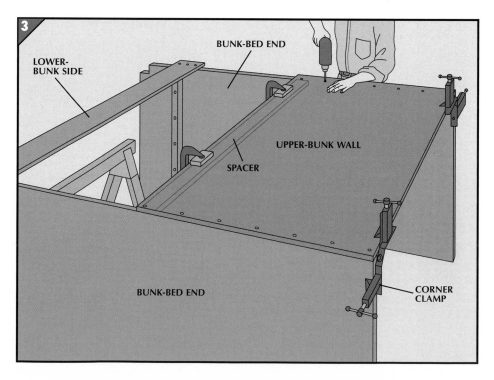

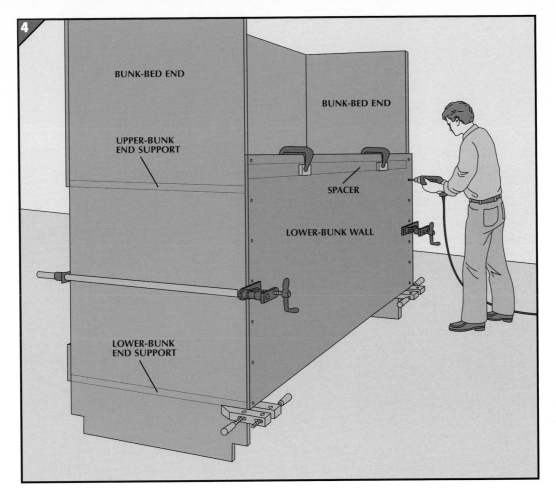

4. Adding the lower-bunk wall.

◆ Cut the lower-bunk wall $78\frac{3}{8}$ inches long from a 4-foot-wide panel of $\frac{3}{4}$-inch plywood and clamp the spacer to the back of it along the top edge.

◆ Install a handscrew clamp on the front edge of each end against the bottom of the lower-bunk end support.

◆ Rest the lower-bunk wall on the clamps with the spacer butted against the bunk-bed ends.

◆ Secure the wall to the bunk ends with bar or pipe clamps, then fasten the wall to the bunk ends with screws and washers *(above)*.

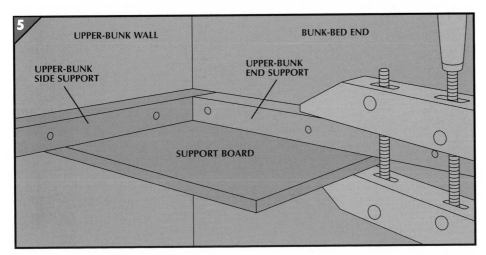

5. Upper-bunk side supports.

◆ Clamp two support boards to the underside of each upper-bunk end support, one against the lower-bunk wall and one against the upper wall.

◆ Cut two 2-by-2s $76\frac{7}{8}$ inches long as side supports for the upper-bunk bottom, then glue and screw *(Step 1)* one to the upper-bunk wall and the other to the lower wall, resting the pieces in position on the support boards as shown at left.

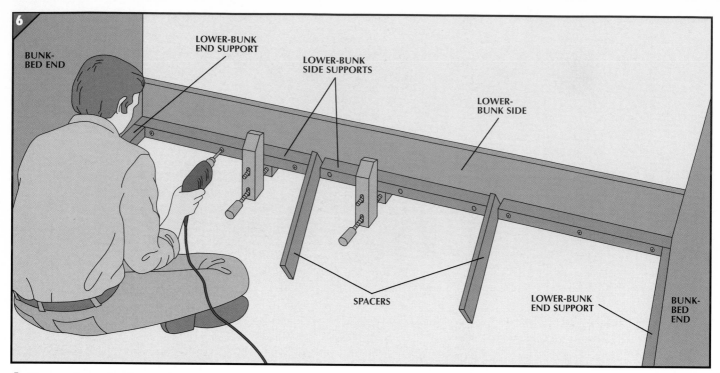

6. Fastening the lower-bunk side supports.

◆ Cut six 2-by-2s $25\frac{1}{8}$ inches long as side supports for the lower-bunk bottom, spread wood glue on one side of two of the pieces, and clamp them along the bottom edge of the lower-bunk side at each end so their edges are at the same level as the end supports attached to the bunk-bed ends.

◆ Clamp and glue a third side support to the lower-bunk side between the first two, separating the pieces with $\frac{3}{4}$-inch plywood spacers. These gaps will later accommodate drawer-support panels *(Step 8)*.

◆ Fasten each side support to the lower-bunk side with three 2-inch No. 10 wood screws *(above)*, then remove the spacers.

◆ Attach side supports to the opposite lower-bunk side in the same way.

7. Mounting the first drawer glide to the bed.

◆ Measure down from the junction of the bottom of the lower-bunk side and the bunk-bed end a distance equal to the depth of the drawer plus $\frac{1}{8}$ inch.

◆ Mark the point *(right)* and from it extend a horizontal line *(dashed line)* across the bunk-bed end to indicate the position for the bottom of the drawer glide.

◆ Screw the drawer glide in place along this line *(page 63, Step 3)*. Since slight adjustments may have to be made later, do not tighten the screws for this or any of the other glides until you are ready to mount them permanently in Step 11.

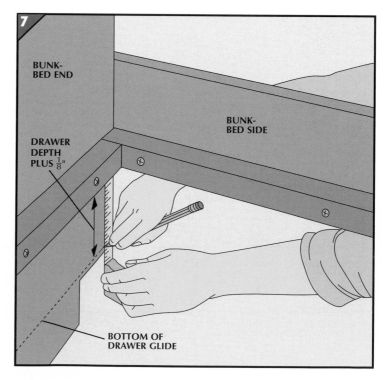

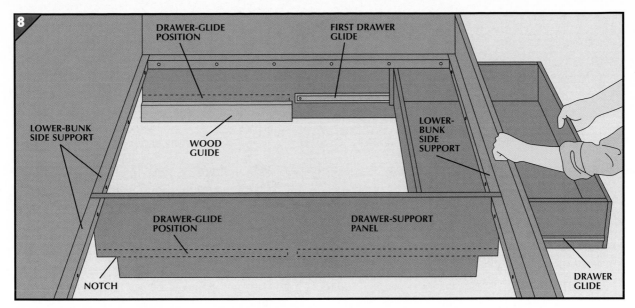

8. Attaching the remaining drawer glides.

◆ Cut a wood guide from $\frac{3}{4}$-inch plywood to the length of the drawer glides. Make the guide as wide as the space between the bottom of the first drawer glide and the floor.

◆ Mount three more glides *(dashed lines)* at the other three corners of the bunk-bed ends, using the wood guide to position them.

◆ Cut two drawer-support panels 41 inches long and $11\frac{3}{8}$ inches wide, and notch them as you did the bunk-bed ends *(page 77, Step 1)*.

◆ Position two drawer glides on each side of the support panels *(dashed lines)*, placing them in the same relationship to the notch as are the glides on the bunk-bed ends.

◆ Into each support panel, drill pilot holes for the screws supplied in the oblong-shaped screw locations of the glides, then slip the panels into the spaces between the lower-bunk side supports.

◆ Position the glides over the pilot holes and screw them loosely in place.

◆ Build six drawers *(page 13)*, sizing them to fit and omitting the false fronts.

◆ Install glides on each drawer *(page 64, Step 4)*.

◆ Check all six drawers for fit *(above)* and adjust the glide positions if needed.

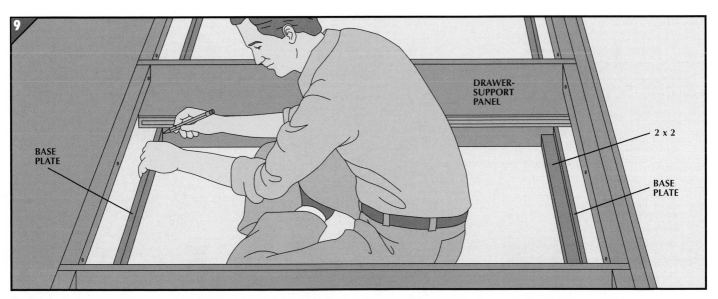

9. Fitting base plates.

◆ Remove the drawers, then cut two base plates 3 inches wide and $78\frac{3}{8}$ inches long.

◆ Drill two pilot holes for $1\frac{1}{2}$-inch No. 10 wood screws at each end of the two plates, centering the holes $\frac{3}{8}$ inch from the edges.

◆ Loosely fasten one base plate in its notches in the bunk-bed ends and mark a line on the back of the plate along the inner side of each notch in the drawer-support panel.

◆ Unscrew the base plate and cut a 2-by-2 to fit between the marked lines.

◆ Spread wood glue on one side of the 2-by-2 and screw it to the base plate's inner face, flush with the bottom edge.

◆ Screw the base plate to the bunk-bed ends.

◆ Repeat the process to mark and mount the other base plate *(above)*.

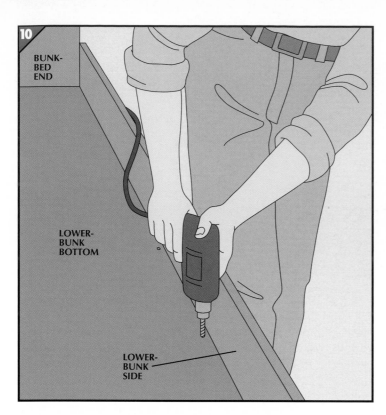

10. Installing the bunk bottoms.
◆ Cut the two bunk bottoms $76\frac{7}{8}$ inches long and 41 inches wide, then place each one on its supports.
◆ Have a helper push against the bunk walls to close any gap between them and the bottoms while you bore pilot holes for 2-inch screws 6 inches to each side of the middle of the long edges, drilling through the bottoms and into the supports beneath *(left)*.
◆ Screw the upper-bunk bottom in place. Remove the lower-bunk bottom for now; it will be fastened later.

11. Drawer-support panels.
◆ Brace the panels temporarily by toenailing two $1\frac{1}{2}$-inch finishing nails through each one into the lower-bunk side supports.
◆ Drill pilot holes for 2-inch screws through each panel into the ends of the 2-by-2s attached to the base plates in Step 9. You may have to drill the holes at an angle.
◆ Drive the screws *(right)*, then pull out the nails.
◆ Put the drawers in place and check that they slide smoothly. Make any necessary adjustments, then remove the drawers and tighten the screws of all the glides. Drive screws in the remaining holes.

BUILDING THE CABINET

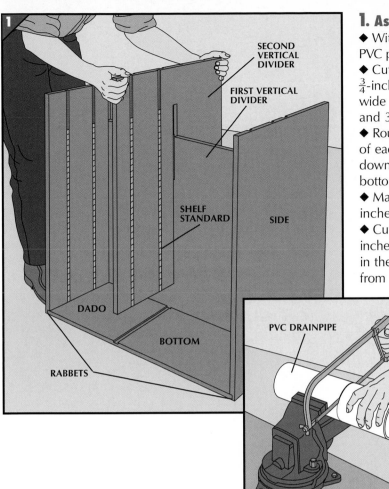

SECOND VERTICAL DIVIDER

FIRST VERTICAL DIVIDER

SHELF STANDARD

SIDE

DADO

BOTTOM

RABBETS

PVC DRAINPIPE

1. Assembling the unit.

◆ With a hacksaw, cut 24 9-inch-long pieces of 4-inch PVC pipe *(inset)*, and smooth the cut ends with sandpaper.

◆ Cut the sides and bottom of the cabinet to size from $\frac{3}{4}$-inch furniture-grade plywood: Make the sides 19 inches wide and 32 inches long, and the bottom 19 inches wide and 30 inches long.

◆ Rout a $\frac{3}{4}$-inch-wide rabbet *(page 10)* along one end of each side, and a $\frac{3}{4}$-inch-wide dado *(page 11)* vertically down their centers; then cut a $\frac{3}{4}$-inch dado across the bottom panel $17\frac{1}{2}$ inches from one end.

◆ Make the first vertical divider $25\frac{5}{8}$ inches tall and 30 inches long.

◆ Cut the second vertical divider 19 inches wide and $31\frac{5}{8}$ inches tall, and use a saber saw to cut a $\frac{3}{4}$-inch-wide notch in the center, running from the bottom to a point 6 inches from the top.

◆ On the inner faces of the sides and on both faces of the second divider, fasten shelf standards *(page 21)* in all the sections, except the one that will house the wine tubes. Offset the standards on opposite sides of the second divider by $\frac{1}{2}$ inch so the dadoes and fasteners will not touch.

◆ Fasten the sides to the bottom with three $1\frac{1}{4}$-inch No. 8 wood screws in each joint, then slip the first divider into its dadoes in the side pieces.

◆ Install the second divider, fitting its notch over the first divider *(left)*, and setting it in the dado in the bottom, then screw the dividers to the sides and bottom.

2. Making and installing the top assembly.

◆ Cut the sides and back of the top assembly 6 inches wide, and long enough to fit snugly around the outside of the cabinet and extend by 6 inches at one end.

◆ With a saber saw, cut a curve at one end of each side piece, then cut drawer openings using the same techniques as for making the cutouts on page 101, Step 1, locating one opening near the curved end of a side and the second near the straight end of the other so that the gap between them will align with the vertical divider.

◆ Drill holes for a 1-inch dowel halfway through the inner faces of the sides near the curved ends, measuring to make sure that the holes will align, then cut the dowel to fit between the holes.

◆ Screw the sides to the back and glue the dowel in its holes, then secure the assembly with two bar clamps, protecting the sides with wood pads.

◆ Cut a drawer-support panel as wide as each drawer cutout and fasten the pieces to the sides so their bottom surfaces are flush with the bottom edges of the sides *(right)*.

◆ Fit the top assembly on the cabinet so its back is flush against one side, then screw it to the sides and the vertical divider through the drawer supports.

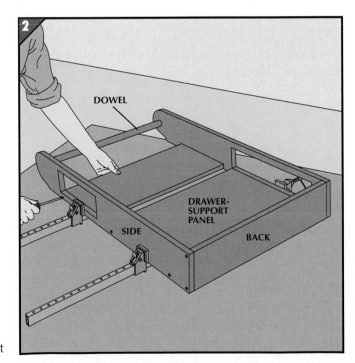

DOWEL

DRAWER-SUPPORT PANEL

SIDE

BACK

ADDING THE FINISHING TOUCHES

1. Making the plinth.

◆ Cut a 2-by-3 into four lengths, mitering the ends at 45-degree angles so the inside corners of the miters will align with the corners of the cabinet.

◆ Along the top edge and inner face of each piece, rout a rabbet $\frac{3}{4}$ inch wide and deep.

◆ Secure the assembly with two bar clamps, then fasten the corners with two screws at each joint *(right)*.

◆ Place the plinth in the desired location of the island, then, with a helper, set the cabinet in the rabbets.

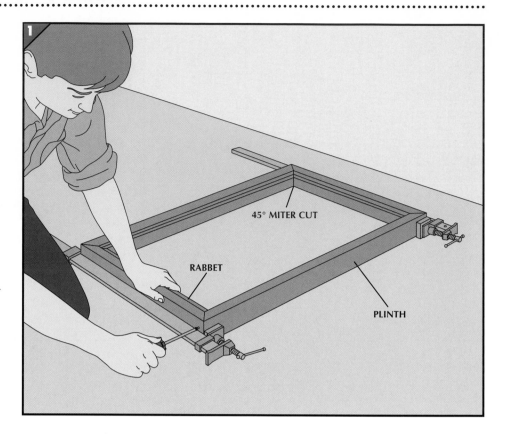

45° MITER CUT

RABBET

PLINTH

LIQUOR-
RACK
CLEAT

ADJUSTABLE
SHELF

2. Shelves, doors, and drawers.

◆ Cut adjustable shelves for the sections of the unit with shelf standards and mount them at the desired heights.

◆ Make a drawer *(page 13)* for each opening in the top assembly.

◆ Cut a door to fit inside the opening in the section next to the wine-storage compartment so its face is flush with the front edges of the side panel and divider. Attach the door to the side panel with flush-mount semiconcealed hinges suitable for frameless cabinets: Fasten the hinges to the inside face of the door in the same manner as the hinges on page 48, Step 1, then set the door inside the opening and screw the other half of the hinge leaves to the front edge of the side panel. For the section behind the wine-storage compartment, mount two doors to meet at the middle of the opening, attaching one to the side panel and the other to the vertical divider. Attach door and drawer handles *(page 13)*.

◆ Cut two pieces of $\frac{3}{4}$- by-$\frac{3}{4}$-inch wood trim to fit as a cleat between the side and vertical divider of the liquor rack, then nail the cleats in place a few inches above each shelf with a $1\frac{1}{2}$-inch finishing nail at each end *(left)*.

3. Adding the wine tubes.

◆ With a caulking gun, apply a bead of silicone caulk along the first PVC tube, stopping the bead $\frac{3}{4}$ inch short of the front end of the tube. Set the tube in the wine-storage compartment so the caulk contacts the bottom panel.

◆ Prepare the remaining tubes in the same way *(right)* with the caulk facing down.

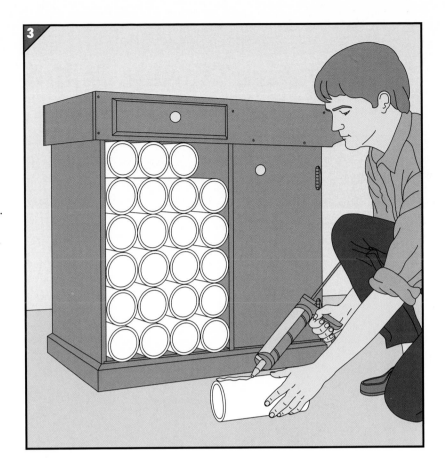

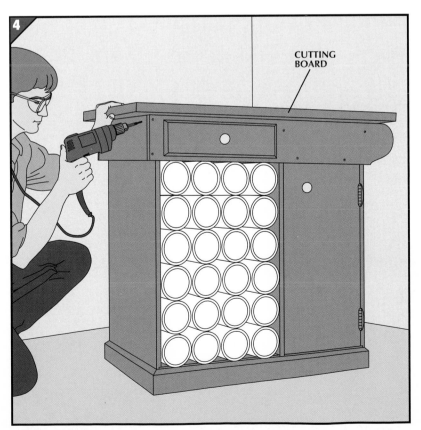

CUTTING BOARD

4. Installing the cutting board.

◆ Spread wood glue on the top edges of the wine island, then position a cutting board 2 inches larger all around than the cabinet on top of the glue.

◆ Fasten the board in place at each corner by driving a $1\frac{1}{2}$-inch screw at an angle through the top assembly into the underside of the board *(left)*.

Innovative Storage in Unfinished Spaces

One way to gain more room for living is to use existing storage areas more efficiently. Custom-built racks and cabinets can bring order to a garage or basement, and a hobby bench can be designed to hold the contents of a workshop while providing a large work surface. For an attic with a hard-to-reach, unfinished floor, simple platforms that roll on casters allow easy access to stored items.

Fastening a storage platform to a wall →

Garages, attics, basements, and utility rooms are perfect places for rough storage. Where appearance is not important, racks and cabinets can be built economically, with inexpensive grades of plywood and lumber replacing furniture-grade panels and boards.

Hanging Platforms: Handy for holding long and unwieldy objects like skis and lumber, or large boxes and bulky items, sturdy platforms can be suspended from exposed joists *(below)*. In a garage, you can hang the racks high enough to accommodate the front of a car parked below them. For damp areas such as a humid basement or a garden shed, the raised shelves will keep belongings high and dry. By varying the lengths of the vertical supports and the spaces between platforms, you can adjust the racks to suit almost any size item.

A Drying Cabinet: Garages or utility rooms with access to heating ducts are ideal for drying wet equipment and clothing in a custom-built cabinet *(pages 114-116)*. Where a duct passes behind a wall, you can cut a hole in the wallboard and duct and install a register.

 TOOLS

Electronic	Electric drill	Drill guide
stud finder	Socket	Compass
Circular saw	wrench	Saber saw
	Carpenter's	Screwdriver
	level	C-clamps

 **MATERIALS**

2 x 4s
Furniture-grade plywood ($\frac{3}{4}$")
Wood trim ($\frac{3}{4}$" x 1")
Dowels ($\frac{3}{4}$", 1", $1\frac{1}{2}$")
Lag screws ($\frac{1}{2}$" x 4")

Wood screws ($1\frac{1}{4}$", $2\frac{1}{2}$" No. 8)
Carriage bolts, washers, and nuts ($\frac{1}{2}$" x 4")
Lead shields
Plexiglass
Heavy-duty plastic screening

SAFETY TIPS

Prevent injury to eyes by wearing goggles when you are using a power tool or hammering.

HANGING PLATFORMS

Suspended shelves.

These heavy-duty platforms have a frame made of 2-by-4 rails covered with $\frac{3}{4}$-inch plywood. The platforms are suspended by vertical supports attached to overhead joists with $\frac{1}{2}$- by 4-inch carriage bolts, and are secured to wall studs with $\frac{1}{2}$- by 4-inch lag screws. The ends of the platforms opposite the wall are reinforced with cleats.

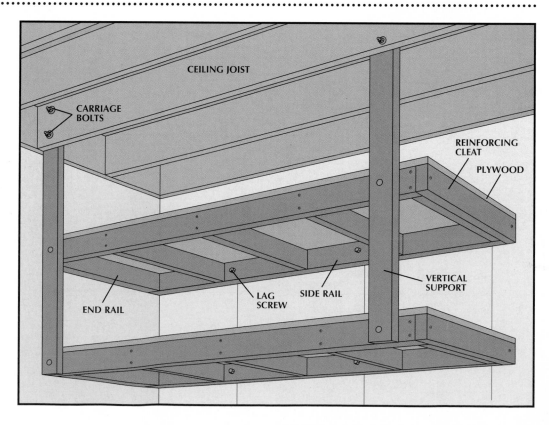

1. Attaching the vertical supports to ceiling joists.

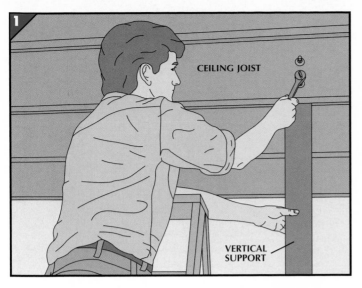

◆ With an electronic stud finder, locate and mark the stud positions on the wall to which you will fasten the platforms. Then, with a carpenter's level, draw a level line along the wall to indicate the bottom of each platform.

◆ Cut two 2-by-4s as vertical supports to fit between the ceiling and the lowest mark on the wall.

◆ On the joist that will hold the supports, mark two points about 5 inches inside each end of the proposed platforms, then drill a hole through the joist at each mark.

◆ Hold a vertical support against the joist and the ceiling, centered on the holes, and mark the hole positions on it.

◆ Drill a hole through the support at each mark, then fasten it to the joist with two $\frac{1}{2}$- by 4-inch carriage bolts, washers, and nuts (left).

◆ Mount the second support to the joist in the same way.

2. Hanging the platforms.

◆ For a masonry wall, drill a level row of holes and insert lead shields (photograph) every 16 inches at the marked position of each platform.

◆ Build the platforms, cutting 2-by-4 side rails to length and end rails to fit between the sides. Join the pieces with two $2\frac{1}{2}$-inch No. 8 wood screws at each corner. Add crosspieces the same size as the end rails for every 12 inches of platform length and a reinforcing cleat 3 inches longer than the end rails across each unsupported end of the platform.

◆ Working with a helper, fasten the topmost platform to the lead shields or wall studs with lag screws.

◆ While the helper holds the platform

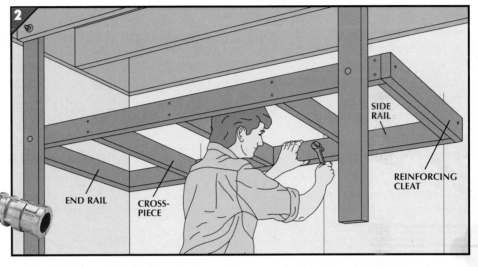

level, drill a $\frac{1}{2}$-inch hole through the side rail into the vertical supports, then attach the platform to the supports with lag screws.

◆ Cut a piece of $\frac{3}{4}$-inch plywood to

cover the frame and fasten it to the rails with a $1\frac{1}{4}$-inch wood screw every 12 inches.

◆ Mount the remaining platforms the same way.

TRICKS OF THE TRADE

Hanging Platforms with Ledgers

If no one is available to help you hang the platforms, you can use 2-by-4 ledgers to support them while you fasten them. When a platform is ready to be mounted, screw a ledger as long as the side rails to the wall just below the platform mark. Prop the platform on the ledger while you fasten it to the vertical supports. After fastening the platform to the wall, remove the ledger or leave it in place.

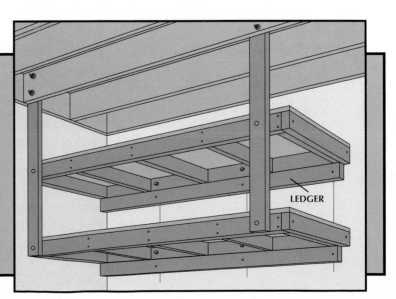

A DRYING CABINET

Anatomy of a drying cabinet.

This floor-to-ceiling cabinet consists of two side panels of $\frac{3}{4}$-inch plywood—18 inches wide, in this example—rabbeted *(page 10)* to accommodate a top piece. Plates 2 inches wide across the top and bottom of the unit add rigidity; the bottom plate sits in rabbets in the back edges of the sides while the top is screwed to the front edges. A $1\frac{1}{2}$-inch dowel hangs 6 inches from the top as a clothes rod, and 48 inches below the dowel a drying shelf of heavy-duty-plastic screening allows warm air to rise above it. Below the shelf, three 1-inch offset dowels in the side pieces serve as drying rods. A 12-inch-wide shoe rack set in dadoes *(page 11)* in the sides has cutouts for shoes or boots to hang upside down. Directly below the shoe rack, ten $\frac{3}{4}$-inch angled dowels 6 inches long can hold small items like socks or gloves. A 12-inch-wide plexiglass panel mounted at an angle directs warm air from a heating vent up through the cabinet. A two-tread folding step stool hinged on a 1-inch dowel can be pulled down to access the top of the cabinet and folded up when not in use *(inset)*.

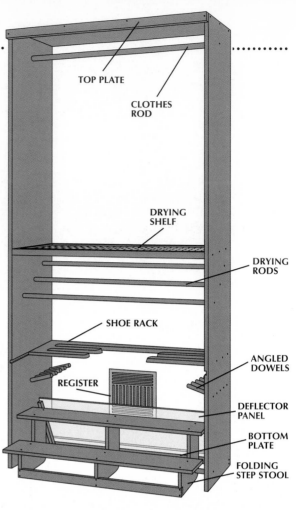

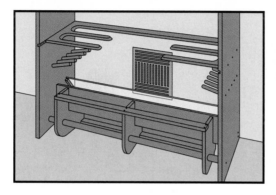

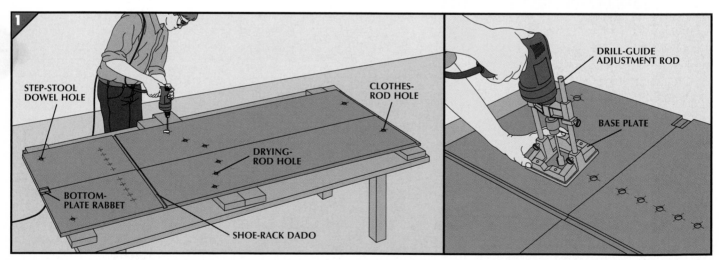

1. Preparing the side pieces.

◆ From $\frac{3}{4}$-inch plywood, cut the sides to size, then set the pieces face-down atop scrap boards on a worktable edge-to-edge with the ends aligned.

◆ Rout a $\frac{3}{4}$-inch rabbet *(page 10)* across the tops of the pieces, a $\frac{3}{4}$-inch dado *(page 11)* for the shoe rack 24 inches from the bottom, and 2-inch-long rabbets along the back edges cut from the bottom for the bottom plate.

◆ Mark the following hole positions on each piece: one hole 3 inches from the top in the center of each side for the coat rack; three holes offset diagonally by $4\frac{1}{2}$ inches, starting 56 inches from the top, for the drying rods; a row of five holes 6 inches below the shoe-rack dado $1\frac{1}{2}$ inches apart for the angled dowels; and one hole 3 inches from the front edge and bottom for the step-stool dowel.

◆ Drill the clothes-rod holes with a $1\frac{1}{2}$-inch spade bit, wrapping a strip of masking tape around it to set the depth at $\frac{3}{8}$ inch as described on page 16, Step 1. Bore the step-stool dowel and drying-rod holes with a 1-inch bit *(above, left)*.

◆ For the angled dowel holes, outfit the drill with a $\frac{3}{4}$-inch bit, mount the tool in a commercial drill guide, and set the adjustment rods to hold the guide's base plate at an angle of 15 degrees. Holding the guide on the surface, align the bit with the mark and drill the hole *(above, right)*.

2. Assembling the drying shelf.

◆ Cut a frame from four plywood strips 2 inches wide to fit inside the cabinet.
◆ Rout a $\frac{3}{4}$-inch rabbet *(page 10)* the length of each piece, then fasten the pieces together with a $1\frac{1}{4}$-inch screw at each corner so the rabbets are facing the interior of the frame.
◆ Trim a 1-inch-wide strip to fit between the sides, lay the piece flat, and fasten it across the middle of the frame *(right)*.
◆ Cut a piece of heavy-duty plastic screening to fit inside the frame.

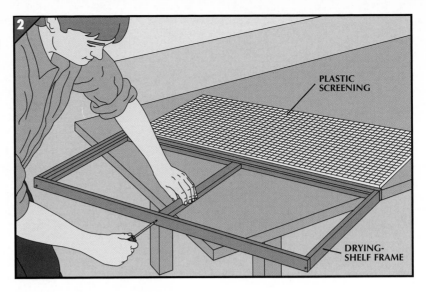

PLASTIC SCREENING

DRYING-SHELF FRAME

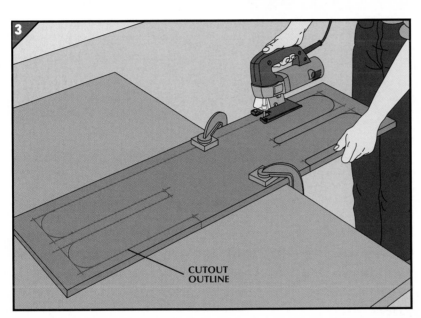

CUTOUT OUTLINE

3. Making the shoe rack.

◆ Cut a piece of plywood 12 inches wide to fit in its dadoes in the sides.
◆ Outline four U-shaped cutouts 4 inches wide and 12 inches long, leaving $1\frac{1}{2}$ inches of wood at each side. Round the outside ends with a compass *(page 104)* adjusted to a radius of 2 inches.
◆ Secure the piece to a worktable with a pair of C-clamps so two of the cutouts overhang the edge.
◆ Set the blade of a saber saw to a 30-degree angle and cut along the outline *(left)*.
◆ Reposition the piece and saw the two remaining cutouts.

4. Installing the deflector panel.

◆ Cut the top, and the top and bottom plates to size.
◆ Fit all the dowels into their holes in one side and add the top and opposite side. Slide the bottom plate into its rabbets and the footwear rack into its dadoes. Screw the top plate to the front edges of the sides, its top edge flush with the top.
◆ To support each edge of the deflector panel, cut a two-piece hanger from $\frac{3}{4}$-inch wood trim: Make one piece 12 inches long and the other 1 inch long, then fasten them together in an L.
◆ Drill a pair of holes for 1-inch No. 8 wood screws through each hanger and position it on the side panel at a 30-degree angle so its top end is 6 inches from the front edge. Fasten the hanger to the side piece *(right)*.
◆ Make the deflector panel by cutting a piece of plexiglass to fit between the cabinet sides to a width of 12 inches.
◆ With a helper, position the cabinet against the wall with a heating register centered between the sides and place the panel on its hangers.

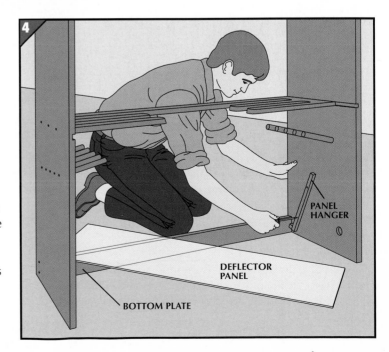

PANEL HANGER

DEFLECTOR PANEL

BOTTOM PLATE

5. Making the step-stool stringers.

◆ To support the treads of the steps, make three stringers—the notched boards at the sides: Cut a piece of $\frac{3}{4}$-inch plywood $11\frac{1}{4}$ inches wide and 12 inches long, then, with a saber saw, cut a 6-inch-square notch from one corner for the lower tread.

◆ With a $1\frac{1}{4}$-inch spade bit, drill a dowel hole through the piece *(Step 1)* 3 inches from the side and 4 inches from the bottom, measuring from the corner opposite the one you notched.

◆ Cut 2-inch notches $\frac{3}{4}$ inch wide to hold the crosspieces *(Step 5)*.

◆ Between the dowel hole and the unnotched corner, mark a pair of intersecting lines 3 inches from one side and 3 inches from the bottom. Set a compass to a radius of 3 inches and, from the intersecting lines, scribe a curve on the surface.

◆ Cut along the line with a saber saw *(right)*.

◆ Make two more stringers using the first as a template.

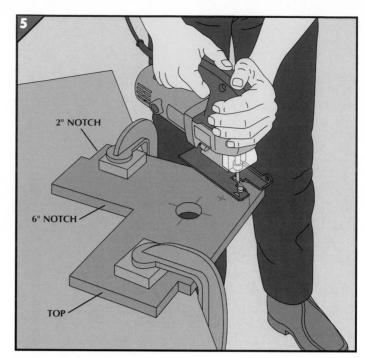

2" NOTCH

6" NOTCH

TOP

6. Assembling the step stool.

◆ Cut two $6\frac{1}{4}$-inch-wide treads 2 inches shorter than the inside dimensions of the cabinet.

◆ On a worktable, position the bottom tread on the outside stringers so it overhangs each stringer by 3 inches. Center the middle stringer between the two others.

◆ Cut two 2-inch-wide crosspieces to fit between the outer sides of the stringers, fit them in their notches, and attach them to each stringer with a pair of $1\frac{1}{4}$-inch screws.

◆ Fasten the bottom tread to each stringer with two screws *(left)*.

◆ Add the top tread.

CROSSPIECE

TREAD

7. Completing the assembly.

◆ Cut a 1-inch dowel $\frac{3}{4}$ inch longer than the inside dimensions of the cabinet and fit it into the holes in the step-stool stringers.

◆ Fit the step-stool dowel in its holes in the sides, spreading them apart gently, if necessary.

◆ Driving a screw at each end, fasten the shoe rack, bottom plate, and all the dowels to the sides *(right)*.

◆ Wedge the drying shelf between the sides 48 inches below the coat rack, check it for level with a carpenter's level, then attach its end frame to each side with three screws.

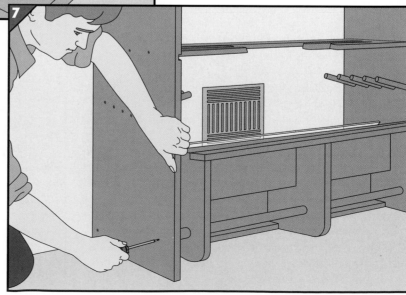

Traveling Platforms for a Cramped Attic

An attic is far too valuable as storage space to be left unused merely because it lacks a floor or has a low roof. Putting in flooring is an expensive, time-consuming job that will solve your storage problem only if the attic is tall enough for you to stand in. You can lay down plywood panels over the joists, but areas far from the trap door will be difficult to reach.

Movable Platforms: A more efficient solution may be to put together trains of movable platforms *(below)* that can give you access even to the space at the ends of the attic. The trains are ideal for use in long, low-roofed attics where the location of the trap door permits them to be several cars long. They may be less effective where space is limited—or where all the available space is within easy reach of the trap door.

Sizing the Units: The width of the platforms will be largely determined by the spacing between the tracks. Do not set the tracks so wide apart that you will have difficulty reaching the far side of the platforms— a spacing of 15 to 20 inches is advisable—and make sure the finished platforms will fit through the trap-door opening.

 CAUTION *When working in an unfinished attic, take care not to step on the ceiling material—it may break.*

 TOOLS

Circular saw
Electric drill
Screwdriver
Carpenter's square
Hammer

MATERIALS

Plywood ($\frac{3}{4}$")
1 x 3s, 2 x 4s
Wood screws
   ($1\frac{1}{4}$" No. 8)
Heavy-duty fencing
   staples
Angle brackets
Nonswiveling
   casters
Clothesline rope
Pulleys (2")
Safety hooks
   and eyes

 SAFETY TIPS

Goggles protect your eyes when you are using a power tool. Add a dust mask and a hard hat when working in an unfinished attic.

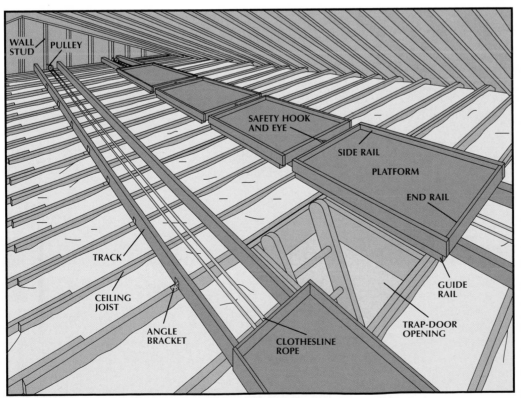

Traveling platforms.
The system at left consists of a train of platforms that travel along a track laid across the ceiling joists. Made of $\frac{3}{4}$-inch plywood, with 1-by-3 side and end rails to keep cargo in place and guide rails to hold them on the track, the cars roll on nonswiveling casters. Safety hooks and eyes keep them hitched together, and a clothesline rope around a pulley fastened to a wall stud at each end of the attic draws them past the trap door for loading and unloading.

WALL STUD | PULLEY | SAFETY HOOK AND EYE | SIDE RAIL | PLATFORM | END RAIL | TRACK | CEILING JOIST | ANGLE BRACKET | CLOTHESLINE ROPE | GUIDE RAIL | TRAP-DOOR OPENING

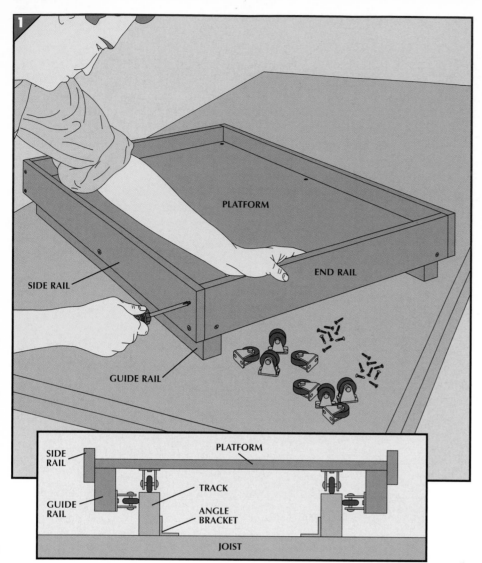

SIDE RAIL

PLATFORM

END RAIL

GUIDE RAIL

SIDE RAIL

GUIDE RAIL

PLATFORM

TRACK

ANGLE BRACKET

JOIST

1. Building the platforms.

◆ For each flatcar, cut a platform to size from $\frac{3}{4}$-inch plywood and two 2-by-4 guide rails to the same length.

◆ Position the plywood on the rails so the outer faces of the boards are flush with the plywood's edges, then drive three $1\frac{1}{4}$-inch No. 8 wood screws through the platform and into the 2-by-4s.

◆ Cut a 1-by-3 side rail 2 inches longer than the guide rails, hold it against the side of one guide rail so it extends beyond the ends and above the platform by 1 inch, then fasten it to the guide rail.

◆ Attach a side rail to the opposite edge of the platform and two end rails between the side pieces, screwing the rails together at the corners *(left)*.

◆ At each corner of the flatcar, mount two nonswiveling casters: one to the underside of the platform to run along the top of the track, and the other to the inner face of the guide rail, flush with the bottom edge, so the wheel will contact the track's outer face *(inset)*.

◆ Make as many of these platforms as you need.

2. Laying the tracks.

◆ Working on a piece of plywood, measure the distance between the attic walls to determine how many 2-by-4s are needed to span its length, cutting some if necessary to match the measurement.

◆ Set the 2-by-4s for the first track across the floor alongside the trap-door opening and between the end walls, using opposite studs as centerpoints for the two tracks. Checking with a carpenter's square that the boards are perpendicular to the ceiling joists, fasten them to every second joist with screws and angle brackets *(right)*.

◆ Anchor the second track, spacing it from the first so the middle of the tracks' top edges will be the same distance apart as the wheels fastened to the underside of the platforms; measure carefully as you go to make sure the two tracks are parallel.

◆ Lay down a second set of tracks on the opposite side of the opening.

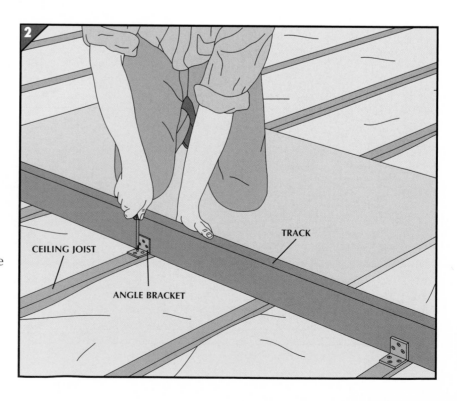

CEILING JOIST

ANGLE BRACKET

TRACK

3. Preparing to join the cars.

◆ Mark the middles of both end rails of each flatcar, then drill a pilot hole for one eye of a safety hook and eye at each mark. For the first and last cars of each train, mark only one rail.

◆ Unclip one eye from its hook, then fasten the hook and eye to a flatcar end rail *(right)*.

◆ Fasten the free eye to the opposite end rail of the same car. Do the same for the rest of the cars, but on the first car, fasten only a hook and eye; and on the last car, attach only an eye.

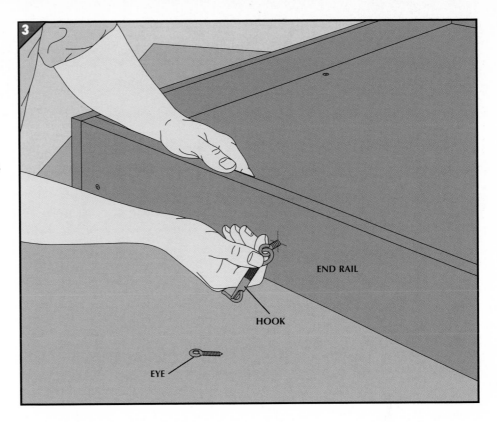

END RAIL

HOOK

EYE

WALL STUD

TRACK

PULLEY

CEILING JOIST

4. Mounting the pulleys.

◆ For each set of tracks, drill a pilot hole for the hook supplied with a 2-inch pulley into each wall stud between the tracks; position the hole midway between the joist and the top of the tracks.

◆ Fasten a hook in each hole, then hang a pulley on each hook.

◆ Run a length of clothesline through one of the pulleys and then through the other *(left)*; tie the ends together to form a loop and leave the knot in the middle of the attic where it will be concealed under one of the platforms; if the knotted part of the rope is left too close to a pulley, it could become jammed when the train is moved.

◆ Put the first car on the tracks and fasten the looped rope to the underside of the platform with a heavy-duty fencing staple.

◆ Position the remaining cars on the tracks with the free eyes facing the hooks, then clip the cars together.

◆ Finish by fastening a second point on the rope to the last car of the train.

An All-Purpose Hobby Bench

Combining ample storage capacity with large and stable work surfaces, the bench shown in these pages is ideal for a wide range of hobbies and can be set up in a garage or basement. Its simple design makes it easy and quick to build.

Planning the Bench: A standard desk is 60 inches long by 30 inches deep and 29 inches high, but you can make the bench with any dimensions that suits your needs. Size the hutch so the drawing board in the open position rests on the front edge of the top and extends a few inches below it. Depending on where the bench will be located, its appearance may not be important; you can make it from either $\frac{3}{4}$-inch furniture-grade plywood or a less expensive grade.

 TOOLS

Circular saw	Bar clamps
Carpenter's square	Router
Electric drill	Screwdriver
C-clamps	Saber saw

 **MATERIALS**

Furniture-grade plywood ($\frac{3}{4}$")	Shelf pins	Door hinges
1 x 2s	Angle brackets (2")	Metal rod
Perforated hardboard ($\frac{1}{8}$")	Wood screws ($\frac{3}{4}$" No. 6, $1\frac{1}{4}$" No. 8)	($\frac{3}{16}$" x 2")
	Metal strapping (8")	Magnetic-catch assembly

 SAFETY TIPS

Wear goggles to protect your eyes when you are using a power tool.

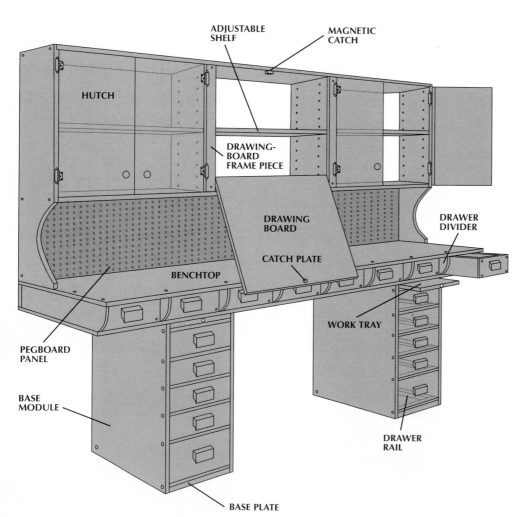

A hobby bench.

The bench at left consists of four individual modules that are built separately, then joined together. The two base modules have a stack of five drawers and a slip-out work tray that glide in and out on U-shaped drawer rails. Drawers separated by curved dividers are sandwiched between base and top panels to form the benchtop, which is fastened to the base modules with angle brackets. The hutch is secured to the benchtop with metal strapping, and a piece of pegboard runs along the back. The top piece of the hutch sits in rabbets *(page 10)* cut in the tops of the sides, and the adjustable shelves in the hutch are supported by shelf pins A drawing board rotates on metal pins in its two frame pieces, and it is kept in the closed position by a magnetic catch attached to the hutch top.

BUILDING THE BASE MODULES

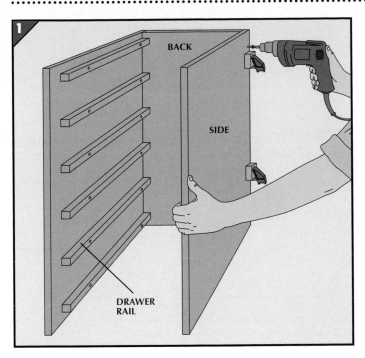

1. Assembling the modules.
◆ From $\frac{3}{4}$-inch plywood or particleboard, trim the back and sides of the modules to size.
◆ For each drawer and slip-out tray, cut two $\frac{3}{4}$-inch-wide drawer rails $2\frac{3}{4}$ inches shorter than the width of the sides.
◆ With two $1\frac{1}{4}$-inch No. 8 wood screws, fasten a rail across the inner faces of the sides at each drawer position *(page 62, Step 1)* $\frac{3}{4}$ inch from the back edge, checking with a carpenter's square that the rails are square on the sides. Locate the last rails 2 inches from the bottom of the sides and 1 inch below the top.
◆ Secure the sides to the back with two bar clamps so the outer face of the back is flush with the ends of the side pieces, then fasten them together *(left)*.

2. Adding the front drawer rails and base plates.
◆ For each drawer, cut a 2-inch-wide plywood strip to fit as a front drawer rail between the sides of the module. Trim an additional strip as a base plate.
◆ Attach the base plate to the sides between the bottom side rail and the bottom of the module so its outer face is inset slightly from the module's front edges.
◆ Fasten drawer rails across the front of the module so they are flush with the side drawer rails and the front edges of the side pieces *(right)*.

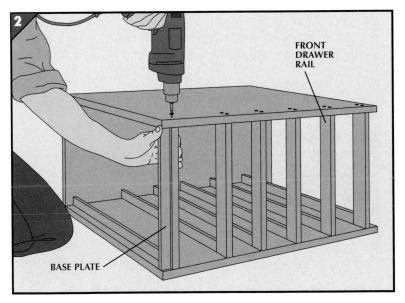

3. Building the drawers.
◆ Make the drawers *(page 13)*, omitting false fronts and pulls.
◆ Cut drawer pulls from 1-by-2s, first making a 30-degree bevel along one edge of the stock using the same techniques for beveling the doors on page 61, Step 1.
◆ Protecting the surface with wood pads, clamp the board to a work-table so you are facing the edge opposite the bevel. Fit a router with a cove bit and, starting near one end, shape the edge *(left)*.
◆ Cut the board into 4-inch lengths and attach them to the drawer fronts *(inset)* with wood glue and screws driven from inside the drawer.

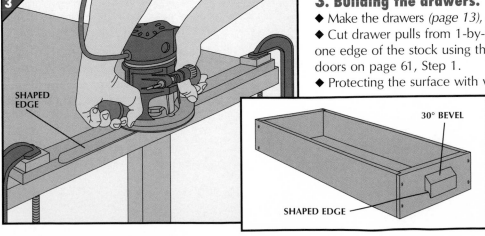

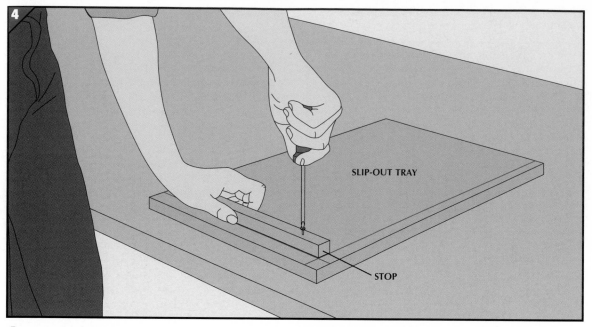

4. Making slip-out trays.

◆ For each tray, trim a piece of plywood to the size of the drawer bottoms.

◆ With a carpenter's square, mark two lines parallel to and 1 inch from adjoining edges of the tray.

◆ Cut a $\frac{3}{4}$-inch-wide strip of plywood 2 inches shorter than the width of the tray and position the strip on the tray so one end is flush with the angle formed by the lines. Fasten it in place as a stop (*above*).

◆ Install the tray in its module opening with the stop facing down; the stop will catch on the front drawer rail below as the tray is opened, keeping it from being pulled all the way out.

◆ Attach a small screw-in drawer pull to the front edge of the tray, centered between the edges.

MAKING THE BENCHTOP

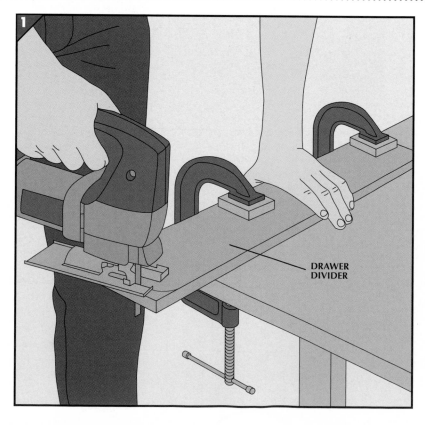

1. Shaping the drawer dividers.

◆ For each drawer in the benchtop section, cut a plywood divider 1 inch longer and $\frac{1}{4}$ inch wider than the sides of the proposed drawers. Make an additional divider to close off the run.

◆ Mark a curve on one side of a divider at one corner, clamp the piece to a worktable, and make the cut with a saber saw (*left*).

◆ Shape the remaining dividers in the same way using the first as a template.

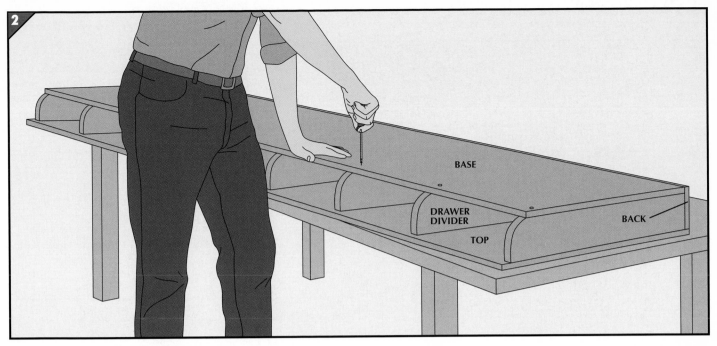

BASE

DRAWER
DIVIDER

BACK

TOP

2. Assembling the benchtop.

◆ Cut the base, top, and back of the benchtop, making all three pieces the same length, but the top 2 inches wider than the base and the back $\frac{3}{4}$ inch wider than the drawer dividers.

◆ Fasten the base and top piece to the back so the back edge of the base is flush with the outer face of the back piece and the top is flush with the upper edge of the back-piece face, using scrap wood to prop up the pieces and driving a screw every 12 inches.

◆ Place the assembly top-down on a worktable, and slip the dividers into position between the top and the base, spacing them equally along the length of the benchtop.

◆ Checking with a carpenter's square that the dividers are perpendicular to the front edge of the top, fasten each one to the base, first along the front *(above)*, then the back.

◆ Turn the assembly over and attach the dividers to the top piece in the same way.

◆ Make the drawers *(page 121, Step 3)*, sizing them so their fronts will be flush with the benchtop base when the drawers are all the way in.

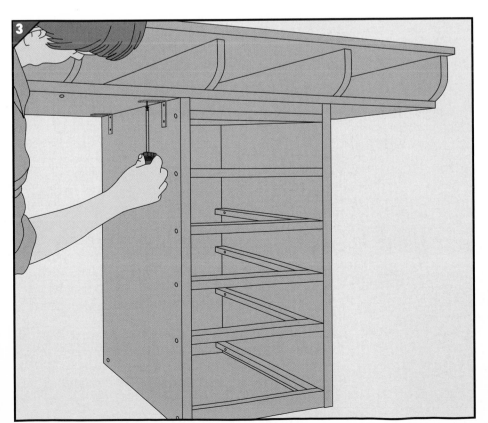

3. Anchoring the benchtop.

◆ Place the base modules in the desired location, then set the benchtop on them. Adjust the placement of the modules so the top extends beyond them by a drawer's width, and check with a carpenter's square that the module sides and the benchtop assembly form right angles at both the front and back.

◆ Fasten the benchtop to each module with two angle brackets on each side of each module, one near the back and one near the front *(left)*.

FASHIONING THE HUTCH

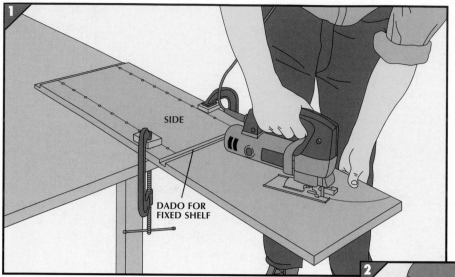

SIDE

DADO FOR
FIXED SHELF

1. Preparing the pieces.
◆ Cut the sides and top of the hutch to size, then rout a dado *(page 11)* across the inner face of each side at the fixed-shelf position.
◆ Rout a rabbet *(page 10)* across the top of each side piece.
◆ Drill two rows of holes for adjustable shelves *(page 21, Step 1)* between the top end and the dado.
◆ Mark the curved cutout on the side's front edge below the dado, clamp the piece to a worktable so the outline overhangs the edge, and make the cut with a saber saw *(left)*.

2. Assembling the hutch.
◆ Stand the top piece on the bench and fit the rabbets in the sides against its end, then fasten the sides to the top so the side's top ends are flush with the top's upper surface.
◆ Cut the fixed shelf as wide as the top and long enough to fit between the dadoes in the sides, slip it into position, and fasten it to the sides with two screws at each end *(right)*.

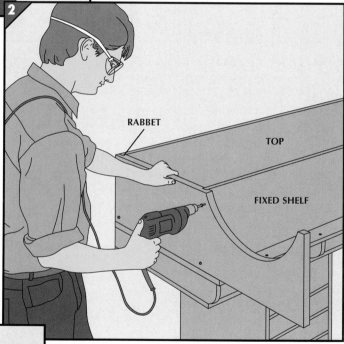

RABBET

TOP

FIXED SHELF

3. Adding the pegboard panel.
◆ Cut a piece of $\frac{1}{8}$-inch pegboard to fit in its place under the hutch.
◆ Cut $\frac{3}{4}$-inch-wide strips for the perimeter of the pegboard as a frame, then attach the pieces flush along the edges of the board with $\frac{3}{4}$-inch No. 6 screws every 16 inches.
◆ Set the hutch on its back and position the pegboard assembly between the sides and flush against the shelf.
◆ With two $1\frac{1}{4}$-inch No. 8 screws per side, fasten the pegboard frame to the hutch so the outer faces of the frame pieces are flush with the back edges of the sides of the hutch *(left)*.

PEGBOARD
PANEL

FRAME
PIECE

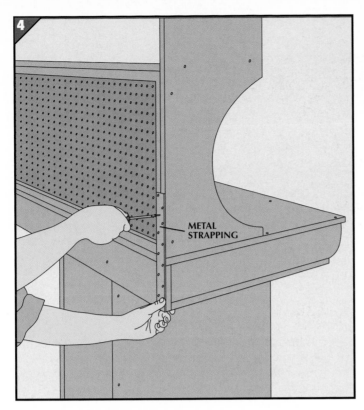

METAL STRAPPING

4. Completing the hutch.

◆ Position the hutch on the benchtop.
◆ For each side of the hutch, hold an 8-inch length of metal strapping across the back edge of the side piece and the benchtop.
◆ Fasten the strapping in place with $\frac{3}{4}$-inch No. 6 screws driven into every second hole *(left)*.
◆ Cut two dividers the same width as the fixed shelf to fit between the shelf and the top of the hutch. Drill holes in both sides of each divider for adjustable shelves *(opposite, Step 1)*. Offset the holes on opposite sides of the dividers by $\frac{1}{2}$ inch so they will not touch.
◆ Checking with a carpenter's square that the dividers are perpendicular to the shelf and top, space them $1\frac{1}{4}$ inches farther apart than the planned width of the drawing board, then fasten only the back ends of the dividers to the top and fixed shelf with $1\frac{1}{4}$-inch No. 8 screws.

5. Mounting the drawing board.

◆ Make 2-inch-wide frame pieces the same length as each divider and, centering them over the dividers' front edges, fasten them with a screw at each end.
◆ Cut the drawing board to fit between the frame pieces and 6 inches longer than the diagonal distance between the front edges of the shelf and the benchtop.
◆ Attach the catch plate of a magnetic-catch assembly to the inner face of the drawing board just below the top edge and centered between the ends.
◆ Fasten the magnetic catch to the underside of the hutch top, centered between the dividers, $\frac{3}{4}$ inch from the top's front edge.
◆ Drill a $\frac{3}{16}$-inch hole 1 inch deep into each edge of the drawing board 2 inches from the end opposite the catch and matching holes in the inner edges of the frame pieces 2 inches above the shelf.
◆ Slip a 2-inch length of $\frac{3}{16}$-inch metal rod into each hole in the drawing board, gently spread the dividers apart, slip the rods into the divider holes *(above)*, push the dividers together, then fasten their front ends to the shelf and hutch top.
◆ Cut and install adjustable shelves, then the doors and hinge one to each divider and one to each side piece *(pages 48-49, Steps 3 and 4)*. Add handles to the doors.

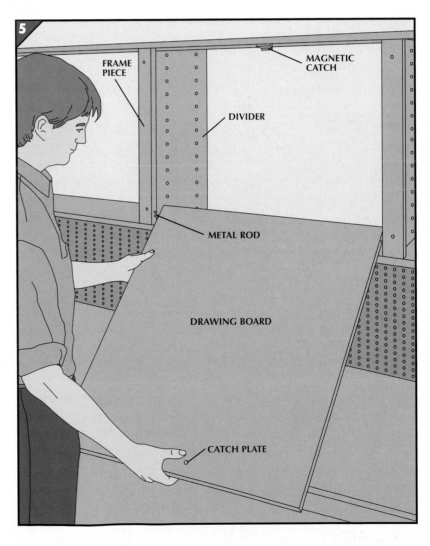

FRAME PIECE

MAGNETIC CATCH

DIVIDER

METAL ROD

DRAWING BOARD

CATCH PLATE

INDEX

TIME LIFE BOOKS

Time-Life Books is a division of Time Life Inc.

TIME LIFE INC.
PRESIDENT and CEO: George Artandi

TIME-LIFE BOOKS
PRESIDENT: Stephen R. Frary
PUBLISHER/MANAGING EDITOR:
Neil Kagan
VICE PRESIDENT, MARKETING:
Steven A. Schwartz

HOME REPAIR AND IMPROVEMENT:
Closets, Space, and Storage
EDITOR: Lee Hassig
DIRECTOR OF MARKETING:
Wells P. Spence
Art Director: Kate McConnell
Associate Editor/Research and Writing:
Karen Sweet
Editorial Assistant: Patricia D. Whiteford

Director of Finance: Christopher Hearing
Directors of Book Production:
Marjann Caldwell, Patricia Pascale
Director of Operations: Betsi McGrath
Director of Photography and Research:
John Conrad Weiser
Director of Editorial Administration:
Barbara Levitt
Production Manager: Marlene Zack
Quality Assurance Manager: James King
Chief Librarian: Louise D. Forstall

ST. REMY MULTIMEDIA INC.
President: Pierre Léveillé
Vice President, Finance: Natalie Watanabe
Managing Editor: Carolyn Jackson
Managing Art Director: Diane Denoncourt
Production Manager: Michelle Turbide

Staff for Closets, Space, and Storage

Series Editors: Marc Cassini, Heather Mills
Art Director: Solange Laberge
Senior Editor: Brian Parsons
Assistant Editor: Jim Hynes
Designers: Jean-Guy Doiron, Robert Labelle
Photographers: Robert Chartier, Martin
Girard, Maryo Proulx, Stéphane Turbide
Editorial Assistants: James Piecowye,
George Zikos
Coordinator: Dominique Gagné
Indexer: Linda Cardella Cournoyer
Systems Director: Edward Renaud
Technical Support: Jean Sirois
Other Staff: Normand Boudreault,
Lorraine Doré, Francine Lemieux,
Robert Paquet

PICTURE CREDITS
Cover: Photograph, Robert Chartier.
Art, Robert Paquet.

Illustrators: La Bande Créative, Gilles Beau-
chemin, Frederic F. Bigio from B-C Graph-
ics, Dale Gustafson, Ken Kay, Lennart
Johnson Designs, Peter McGinn, Kurt
Ortell, Jacques Perrault

Photographers: **End papers:** Glenn Moores
and Chantal Lamarre. **17, 21, 28, 29,
48, 61, 63, 65, 113:** Glenn Moores and
Chantal Lamarre.

ACKNOWLEDGMENTS
The editors wish to thank the following indi-
viduals and institutions: Jeff Asher and Colin
Ericksen, Euro-Limited, High Point, NC.;
Birchall & Associates, Mississauga, Ont.;
DeWalt Industrial Tool Company, Richmond
Hill, Ont.; Jon Eakes, Montreal, Que.; Karl
Marcuse, Montreal, Que.; Richelieu Hard-
ware Ltd., Montreal, Que.; Stanley Tools, a
Division of Stanley Canada Inc., Burlington,
Ont.; ToolTrend Limited, Concord, Ont.;
Wolfcraft Inc., Itasca, IL; Woodworkers' Store,
Medina, MN

**Library of Congress
Cataloging-in-Publication Data**
Closets, space, and storage / by the editors
of Time-Life Books.
p. cm. — (Home repair and improvement)
Includes index.
ISBN 0-7835-3922-3
1. Cabinetwork. 2. Storage in the home.
3. Built-in furniture.
I. Time-Life Books. II. Series.
TT197.C584   1998
643'.5—dc21   98-3754